westermann

W0469315

CAMDEN MARKET

7

Arbeitsbuch Inklusion

CAMDEN MARKET 7

Arbeitsbuch Inklusion

Autorin: Christina Wolkenhauer (Rosenow)
Unter Mitwirkung von: Henriette Vahle und Daniel Walker
Fachliche Beratung: Sandra Schünemann und Miriam Skott

Zusatzmaterialien zu Camden Market 7

Materialien für Lehrerinnen und Lehrer

- Textbook für Lehrkräfte 7 (ISBN 978-3-14-149149-4)
- Materialien für Lehrkräfte 7 (ISBN 978-3-14-149150-0)
- Differenzierende Kopiervorlagen 7 (ISBN 978-3-14-149155-5)
- Lernerfolgskontrollen 7 (ISBN 978-3-14-149152-4)
- CD für Lehrkräfte 7 (ISBN 978-3-14-149153-1)
- DVD für Lehrkräfte 7 (ISBN 978-3-14-149154-8)
- Online-Diagnose zu Camden Market 7 www.onlinediagnose.de

Materialien für Schülerinnen und Schüler

- Textbook 7 (ISBN 978-3-14-149138-8)
- Workbook 7 (ISBN 978-3-14-149139-5)
- Interaktive Übungen 7 (ISBN 978-3-14-149368-9)
- Klassenarbeitstrainer 7 (ISBN 978-3-14-149142-5)
- Grammatiktrainer 7 (ISBN 978-3-14-149143-2)
- Wortschatztrainer 7 (ISBN 978-3-14-149392-4)
- Let's talk 7 (ISBN 978-3-14-149146-3)
- Let's write 7 (ISBN 978-3-14-149402-0)

Das digitale Schulbuch und digitale Unterrichtsmaterialien für Schülerinnen und Schüler und für Lehrkräfte finden Sie in der BiBox – dem digitalen Unterrichtssystem passend zum Lehrwerk. Mehr Informationen über aktuelle Lizenzen finden Sie auf www.bibox.schule.

www.westermann.de/camden-market

westermann GRUPPE

Druck A[1] / Jahr 2022
Alle Drucke der Serie A sind im Unterricht parallel verwendbar.

Redaktion: Henriette Vahle und Daniel Walker
Vokabelanhang: Lisa Hambrecht, Köln
Illustrationen: Ulf Marckwort, Kassel
Umschlaggestaltung: LIO Design GmbH, Braunschweig
Layout: JANSSEN KAHLERT Design & Kommunikation GmbH, Hannover
Druck und Bindung: Westermann Druck GmbH, Georg-Westermann-Allee 66, 38104 Braunschweig

ISBN 978-3-14-**149141**-8

Camden Market Rallye

Mit der Camden Market Rallye kannst du dein Englischbuch kennenlernen. Du beantwortest dabei Fragen zu den verschiedenen Teilen des Buches. Die Buchstaben ergeben ein Lösungswort.

1 Auf Seite 5 werden die Hauptfiguren von Camden Market vorgestellt. Wer hat zwei Schwestern?

R Sandeep E Ben

2 Wie viele Kapitel (*Themes*) gibt es?

L sechs N fünf

3 Jedes *Theme* hat ein Hauptthema. Blättere *Theme* 5 durch. Worum geht es?

G um Ferien und Reisen
I um Sport und Ernährung

4 Worum geht es in der Land & Leute Box in *Theme* 5?

L um Loch Ness
T um Museen

5 Neben Aufgabe 14 in *Theme* 2 findest du dieses Symbol: ✎
Was sollst du hier tun?

A lesen I schreiben

6 Auf den Seiten 98 bis 102 findest du für jedes *Theme* eine *Wordbank*. Was sollst du hier tun?

S wichtige Wörter und Sätze zum *Theme* sammeln
K Texte schreiben und vortragen

7 Auf den Seiten 103 bis 108 kannst du Redemittel nachschlagen. Was wird in Nummer 13 auf Seite 105 erklärt?

H So kannst du sagen, was du gerade machst.
M So kannst du Fragen stellen.

__	__	__	__	__	__	__
1	2	3	4	5	6	7

Hast du das Rätsel gelöst? Klasse!

Viel Spaß mit Camden Market!

Symbole und Verweise

Diese Dinge übst du:

Hören Sprechen Lesen Schreiben

Hier gibst du Informationen aus einem englischen Text auf Deutsch weiter.

4 Diesen Text kannst du dir anhören. Die Hörtexte werden online angeboten. Gib den Webcode **WES-149141-001** auf www.westermann.de/webcode ein.

Wörter in blauer Schrift kannst du in deinen eigenen Sätzen austauschen.

Diese Kästchen werden dir im Buch begegnen:

Hier erfährst du interessante Dinge über Großbritannien.

Hier findest du Tipps zu den Aufgaben.

Hier findest du wichtige Redemittel.

Diese Kids wirst du wiedertreffen:

Megan McGregor
- 13 years old
- lives with her mum
- has got a half brother
- has got a dog
- likes rugby and animals

Sandeep Chopra
- 13 years old
- has got a sister and a brother
- parents have got a shop
- likes music and football

Jasmine Bolt
- 13 years old
- has got a brother
- has got a cat and a guinea pig
- likes basketball and taking photos

Ben Hancock
- 14 years old
- has got two sisters and a brother
- has got two budgies
- likes drawing and computers

Theme 1

Are you fit?

In diesem *Theme* beschäftigst du dich mit ...

- **Sport und Fitness,**
- **Wohltätigkeitsveranstaltungen,**
- **Schulessen und gesunder Ernährung,**
- **Essensbestellung im Restaurant.**

☐ Jumping up and down

☐ Balancing on one leg

1 Test your fitness

a) Match the pictures and the exercises.
Ordne die Bilder den Übungen zu.

b) Do the exercises with a partner.
Macht die Übungen zu zweit.

- [ ] Running up and down 20 steps quickly
- [ ] Holding a can
- [ ] Walking backwards
- [ ] Pressing my back against a wall

c) Talk about the exercises with a partner. Sprecht zu zweit über die Übungen.

Holding a can was easy.

... was really hard.

... was no problem.

... was too hard.

2 Favourite sports

a) **Read the article in the Haverstock school magazine.**
Lies den Artikel in der Schülerzeitung von Haverstock.

Tell us: What's your favourite sport?

I like hockey

I really like playing hockey. It's my favourite sport because it's exciting and fast. We don't need helmets or special clothes. I train on Mondays and Thursdays.
I enjoy playing outside.
Telisha, 15

Skateboarding

Skateboarding is a great sport. There's a skate park near my house and I meet my friends there after school. We practise different tricks and have a lot of fun together.
Jai, 11

b) **Complete the table. Use the help in the box below.**
Vervollständige die Tabelle. Nutze die Hilfe im Kasten unten.

name	how old?	what sport?	when?	why?

hockey | 11 | exciting and fast | Telisha | skateboarding | 15 | lots of fun | after school | Jai | on Mondays and Thursdays

4 My favourite sport

a) **Find 7 sports in the wordsearch.** Finde 7 Sportarten im Rätsel.

F	Y	C	Y	C	L	I	N	G	T	N	R
O	D	H	S	A	Q	J	S	F	L	H	U
J	G	Y	M	N	A	S	T	I	C	S	N
U	N	E	S	R	I	D	I	N	G	D	N
D	G	B	F	U	V	D	T	M	H	V	I
O	F	O	O	T	B	A	L	L	G	F	N
L	E	S	W	I	M	M	I	N	G	D	G

b) **Fill in the table.** Fülle die Tabelle aus.

My favourite sport is	swimming | football | cycling | running | riding | gymnastics | ...	swimming
I like it because	it's fast | it's fun | I meet my friends | I play in a team | ...	
You need	a ball | a basket | a net | a goal | a hockey stick | swimwear | a horse | a bike | a helmet | ...	
I train	every Monday | after school | at the weekend | ...	
I do/play it	inside | outside | in a park | at the sports centre | ...	

c) **Write the text on a piece of paper. Then present it.**
Schreibe den Text auf ein Blatt Papier. Dann präsentiere ihn.

5 Sports people

a) **Who is your favourite sports person or e-sports person?**
Wer ist dein Lieblingssportler/deine Lieblingssportlerin?

My favourite sports person is ...

b) **Read the fact files and choose one person.**
Lies die Steckbriefe und suche dir eine Person aus.

I like ...

FACT FILE
Name: Pernille Harder
Age: 29
Country: Denmark
Sport: football
Other information:
was the best European player in women's football in 2018 and 2020, plays in the national team of Denmark

FACT FILE
Name: Spencer "Gorilla" Ealing
Age: 25
Country: England
Sport: FIFA
Other information:
is one of the best FIFA players in the world, was world champion in 2017

c) **Present your sports person.** Stelle deinen Sportler/deine Sportlerin vor.

My sports person is ______________________.
He/She is ____________ years old.
He/She comes from ______________________.
He/She plays ______________________.
I like him/her because he/she ______________________.

d) **Now find information about your favourite sports person. Make a fact file on a piece of paper.**
Finde nun Informationen über deinen Lieblingssportler/deine Lieblingssportlerin. Erstelle einen Steckbrief auf einem Blatt Papier.

FACT FILE
Name:
Age:
Country:
Sport:
Other information:

7 A sports event

a) Schau dir das Poster an. Beantworte die Fragen von jemandem, der kein Englisch versteht.

1. Welche Teams treten im Freundschaftsspiel gegeneinander an?
2. Welche Farbe soll man tragen, um bei der Spendensammlung zu helfen?
3. Was kostet der Eintritt?
4. Wann findet das Freundschaftsspiel statt?
5. Wo findet es statt?

b) Listen to Jasmine and Ben. Underline the words you hear. 1
Höre Jasmine und Ben zu. Unterstreiche die Wörter, die du verstanden hast.

e-sports event | friendly match | football | charity run | running |
Megan and Sandeep | biology teacher | English teacher |
blue trainers and shorts | Megan and Ben | red scarf | handball |
red jacket and trainers | Red Nose Day | Black Friday | red cap

c) Listen again. Answer the questions. Höre erneut zu. Beantworte die Fragen.

1. What did they do to raise money? friendly match
2. What did they play? ________
3. Who played in the students' team? ________
4. Who was the goalkeeper? ________
5. What did Ben wear? ________
6. What did Jasmine wear? ________
7. What day is it? ________

8 A friendly match

a) Look at the picture. What can you see?
Sieh dir das Bild an. Was kannst du sehen?

b) Read the article. Lies den Artikel.

Du kannst dir den Text auch anhören. 2

A friendly match for charity

Last Sunday the students of Haverstock School played against their teachers in a friendly match for Red Nose Day.

The players wore red noses and the fans all wore something red, too.

It was a great day and the teams raised about £240 for charity.

When the match started at 3:30 p.m., the students were chanting "Let's go, students! Let's go!"

And after only five minutes, team captain Megan McGregor scored the first goal!

But the friendly match ended in a draw.

It was an exciting match and everyone was happy that they raised so much money for charity!

c) Read the article again. Underline the correct answers.
Lies den Artikel noch einmal. Unterstreiche die richtigen Antworten.

1. The game was last Saturday / last Sunday.
2. It was a friendly match for Red School Day / Red Nose Day.
3. The players wore red noses / red shorts.
4. They raised £260 / £240 for charity.
5. The match started at 3:30 / 2:30.
6. The match ended in a draw / with a winning goal for the students.

LAND & LEUTE

Red Nose Day
In Großbritannien gibt es den so genannten *Red Nose Day*. Leute spenden Geld für einen wohltätigen Zweck und tragen eine rote Plastiknase.
Viele berühmte Menschen machen mit.
Das Geld ist zum Beispiel für Hungernde, Obdachlose und Kranke.

Gibt es an deiner Schule auch Wohltätigkeitsveranstaltungen?

9 Target task: Your sports event to raise money

a) **Your school wants to raise money for charity. What will you do? Work with a partner. Collect ideas. Underline or complete.**
Deine Schule möchte Spendengelder sammeln. Was wollt ihr machen? Arbeitet zu zweit. Sammelt Ideen. Unterstreicht oder ergänzt.

What do you want to do?
a football match
a handball match
a sponsored run
an e-sports event
a flea market
a cake sale
...

Where will it take place?
at the sports ground
in the playground
in the classrooms
in the sports hall
...

When will you do it?
in summer
in winter
at the weekend
in the afternoon
...

b) **Complete the text.** Ergänze den Text.

Our idea is to raise money for charity.
We want to organise ______________________.
The event will take place ______________________.
It will be ______________________.

c) **Present your ideas.** Stellt eure Ideen vor.

1 In the cafeteria

a) Look at the picture. What can you see?
Sieh dir das Bild an. Was kannst du sehen?

Du kannst dir die Wörter in b) auch anhören. 3

b) What food and drink is there in the picture? Circle the correct words.
Welche Speisen und Getränke sind im Bild zu sehen? Kreise die richtigen Wörter ein.

1. chips | 2. potatoes | 3. apples | 4. tomatoes | 5. ketchup | 6. eggs | 7. fruit juice | 8. lemonade | 9. water | 10. salad | 11. spaghetti | 12. bananas

c) Number the pictures. Nummeriere die Bilder.

2 A survey

Ask your classmates about their breakfast.
Befrage deine Klassenkameraden über ihr Frühstück.

Do you …

1. have breakfast before school?
2. eat fruit every day?
3. bring a snack to school?
4. eat vegetables once a day?
5. eat sweets every day?

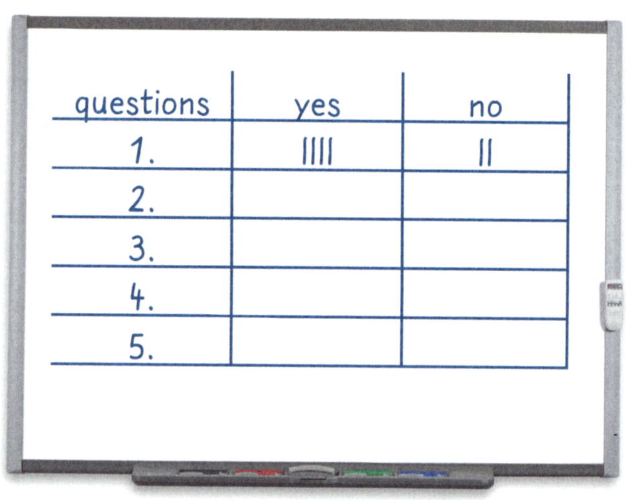

3 Good for you?

a) Listen and repeat. Höre zu und wiederhole. 4

smoothie

cereal

dark chocolate

sugary drinks

spinach

yoghurt

b) Look at the pictures. What is healthy? Circle.
Schau dir die Bilder an. Was ist gesund? Kreise ein.

c) Talk to a partner. Sprecht zu zweit.

I think yoghurt is healthy.

I think ... are healthy.

d) Read the tips. Match them with the pictures.
Lies die Tipps. Ordne sie den Bildern zu.

1. Start the day with a good breakfast.
2. Be careful! Most cereals and some smoothies have too much sugar.
3. Eat five portions of fruit and vegetables every day.
4. Sugary drinks are bad for your health – and your teeth!
5. Drink lots of water.

4 Lunch at school

a) Listen to Jack. What does he like for lunch? Circle. 5
Höre Jack zu. Was mag er zum Mittagessen? Kreise ein.

meat | fish | rice | chips | burgers | potatoes | vegetables | desserts | salads

b) Now listen to Shima and circle. Höre jetzt Shima zu und kreise ein.

vegetable lasagne | burgers | chips | vegetables | fish | salads | fruit | spaghetti | rice | ice cream | potatoes

c) Listen again and check. Höre erneut zu und kontrolliere.

d) Find the pairs. Draw lines. Finde die Paare. Verbinde.

yummy/tasty	gut
good	widerlich
delicious	lecker
not so good	köstlich
disgusting	nicht so gut

e) Talk to a partner about the food at your school.
Sprecht zu zweit über das Essen an eurer Schule.

I think the food at our school is OK/good/yummy/delicious/bad/...

I like the fruit.

I don't like the rice.

6 Very British?

a) What is their favourite food? Read the answers.
Was ist ihr Lieblingsessen? Lies die Antworten.

Katie

I'm a vegetarian.
I like green tea and Thai food without meat and fish.
It's so good!

I love curry. My friend from India makes the best curry!

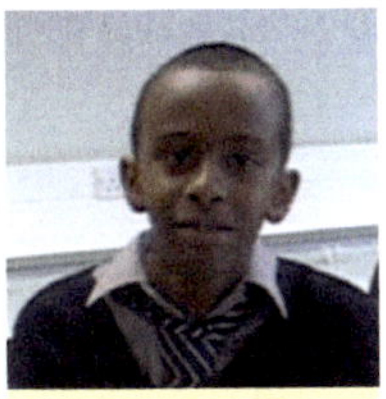

Yusuf

Taylor

My favourite food is Italian.
I like all kinds of pasta and pizza.

My favourite food is fast food – burgers and chips and a cola.

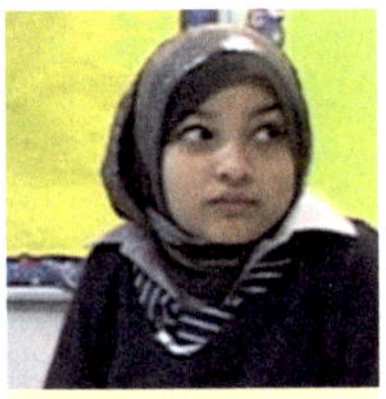

Safia

b) Underline all the food and drink words. Unterstreiche alle Gerichte und Getränke.

c) Read the sentences. Tick true or false.
Lies die Sätze. Mache ein Häkchen bei richtig oder falsch.

	true	false
1. Katie loves Thai food with fish.	☐	☐
2. Taylor likes pasta and pizza.	☐	☐
3. Safia drinks cola and likes burgers and chips.	☐	☐
4. Yusuf loves pasta.	☐	☐

8 A menu

a) **Look at the menu. Which dishes are new to you?**
Sieh dir die Speisekarte an. Welche Gerichte sind neu für dich?

b) **Lies die Speisekarte. Erkläre sie jemandem, der kein Englisch versteht.**

Das Restaurant heißt ...
Es gibt ...
Sie haben ...
Schokokuchen kostet ...

Yummy!
The best place to eat in Camden

Starters

Soup of the day	£4.75
House salad	£4.95
Garlic bread	£2.50

Main courses

Chicken curry	£12.25
Roast beef and Yorkshire pudding	£13.50
Fish and chips	£12.50
Vegetable lasagne	£11.95

Desserts

Chocolate cake	£4.60
Apple crumble	£4.85
Ice cream	£4.50

Drinks

Lemonade or water	£2.65
Juice (orange or apple)	£2.85
Coffee or tea	£2.00

9 Eating out

a) **Listen. Who is talking? Where are they? Underline.** 6
Höre zu. Wer spricht? Wo sind sie? Unterstreiche.

Ben | Jasmine | Megan | Sandeep | Megan's mum | Megan's dad

in a cafeteria | in a restaurant | in a shop

b) Listen again and read along. Underline all the food and drink words.
Höre erneut zu und lies mit. Unterstreiche alle Gerichte und Getränke.

It is Friday evening. Megan's mum has taken her daughter and Ben to Yummy, a nice little restaurant in Camden.

Waiter:	Are you ready to order?
Megan:	Yes, let's start. I'll have the vegetable lasagne and an orange juice, please.
Waiter:	Good. What would you like, madam?
Mrs McGregor:	I'd like the roast beef and Yorkshire pudding, please.
Waiter:	Sure. And what would you like to drink?
Mrs McGregor:	Just some sparkling water, please.
Waiter:	Certainly. And what about you?
Ben:	I'll have the chicken curry and an apple juice, please.
Waiter:	OK. Would you like anything else?
Mrs McGregor:	No, that's everything, thank you.
Waiter:	Great, I'll be back in a minute with your drinks.

An hour later ...

Waiter:	Did you enjoy the food?
Megan:	Yeah, we did. It was really yummy.
Mrs McGregor:	Could you bring the bill, please?
Waiter:	I'll be right with you, madam.

c) Answer the questions. Beantworte die Fragen.

1. What did Megan order to drink? ______________________
2. What did Mrs McGregor order? ______________________
____
3. What did Ben order to drink? ______________________
4. Who said: "Did you enjoy the food?"? ______________________

11 Choose an activity

- **Listen to the poem and read along. Work in groups of 4. Choose one line and learn it by heart. Then present the poem.** 7
  Höre dir das Gedicht an und lies mit. Arbeitet zu viert. Wählt eine Zeile und lernt sie auswendig. Dann tragt das Gedicht vor.

I eat my peas with honey.
I've done it all my life.
It makes the peas taste funny
but it keeps them on my knife.

- **Find 5 things ...** Finde 5 Dinge ...

1. in a fridge: milk, ____________________
2. in a restaurant: menu, ____________________

12 In a restaurant

a) **Read the sentences. Find the correct order and number.**
Lies die Sätze. Finde die richtige Reihenfolge und nummeriere.

1	Are you ready to order?
3	What would you like to eat?
5	OK. Anything to drink for you?
7	Here you are. Enjoy your meal.
9	Would you like a dessert?
11	That's £10.50.
13	Thank you. Goodbye.

	I'll have a salami pizza, please.
	No, thank you. Can you bring the bill, please?
	Thank you.
	Here you are.
2	Yes, I am.
	Goodbye.
	I'd like a bottle of water, please.

b) **Listen and check.** Höre zu und vergleiche. 8

c) **Read out the dialogue with a partner.** Lest den Dialog zu zweit.

14 Target task: A scene at a restaurant

a) **Work in small groups. Make up a scene at a restaurant.**
Arbeitet in kleinen Gruppen. Denkt euch eine Szene in einem Restaurant aus.

b) **What's on your menu? Collect food and drink words.**
Was ist auf eurer Speisekarte? Sammelt Speisen und Getränke.

Our menu

Food	£	Drinks	£
______		______	
______		______	
______		______	
______		______	

c) **Complete the dialogue.** Vervollständige den Dialog.

Are you ready to order?	Yes, I am.
What would you like to eat?	I'll have ______, please.
OK. Anything to drink for you?	I'd like ______, please.
Here you are. Enjoy your meal.	Thank you.
Would you like a dessert?	Yes, ______, please.
Here you are.	Can I have the bill, please?
That's £______.	Here you are.
Thank you. Goodbye.	Goodbye.

d) **Practise and act out your scene.** Übt eure Szene und spielt sie vor.

1 Weekend plans

What are you going to do at the weekend? Talk to a partner.
Was hast du am Wochenende vor? Sprecht zu zweit.

What are you going to do this weekend?

I'm going to visit my grandma.

Mit *going to* sprichst du über Pläne in der Zukunft:
I'm going to play football next Sunday.
She is going to visit her dad at the weekend.

read a book

watch a film

meet friends

play football

go to the cinema

go swimming

2 That's cool!

a) Listen and read along. Höre zu und lies mit. 9

Jasmine: We could have a Halloween party at my house at the weekend.
Megan: Great idea! I'm going to dress up as a vampire.
Jasmine: And I'm going to wear my spooky witch costume.
Ben: I don't know what I'll wear yet. But we'll need a jack-o'-lantern.
Sandeep: Yeah, that's right. I'm going to bring a pumpkin.
Megan: That's great! We also need good music. I'm going to make a playlist.
Ben: Thanks, Megan. And we could watch a scary film. I'm going to ask my brother if he knows a good one.
Jasmine: Yeah, cool! And don't forget about food and drinks, guys. I've seen some great recipes for Halloween muffins and cakes ... and blood-red party punch.

b) Underline the friends' plans. Unterstreiche die Pläne der Freunde.

c) **Who is going to do what? Draw lines. Then read out the sentences.**
Wer wird was machen? Verbinde. Dann lies die Sätze vor.

is going to dress up as a vampire.

is going to bring a pumpkin.

is going to choose a scary film.

is going to wear her witch costume.

is going to make a playlist.

3 Plans for Halloween

Look at the pictures. Then complete the sentences.
Sieh dir die Bilder an. Dann vervollständige die Sätze.

decorate the living room | look for good music | try on Halloween costumes | make muffins | carve a pumpkin

Megan is going to ______________________________

Jasmine and Sandeep are going to ______________________________

Ben is going to ______________________________

Jasmine is going to ______________________________

Ben and Jasmine are going to ______________________________

5 The party can begin

a) Look at the picture. Say what you see.
Sieh dir das Bild. Sage, was du siehst.

b) Find these things in the picture and circle them.
Finde diese Dinge im Bild und kreise sie ein.

a black cat | a pumpkin | a black balloon | party punch | a salad | a witch

c) Read the sentences. What have the friends already done? Match.
Lies die Sätze. Was haben die Freunde schon erledigt? Ordne zu.

1. Jasmine and Megan have put up lots of orange and black balloons.
2. Sandeep has brought a really big pumpkin.
3. Ben and Jasmine have made muffins and much more.
4. The friends have chosen lots of cool songs for their playlist.
5. The girls have put on their costumes.
6. Sandeep has put on some face paint.

d) Read c) again. Make correct sentences. Draw lines.
Lies c) erneut. Bilde richtige Sätze. Verbinde.

I have ...
He has ... / She has ...
They have ...

Sandeep —		made	muffins, a cake, ...
Jasmine and Megan	has	brought	some face paint.
Ben and Jasmine	have	put up	lots of cool songs.
The friends		put on	their costumes.
The girls		chosen	a pumpkin.
			balloons.

6 Already done?

What has Jason already done? Write sentences.
Was hat Jason schon erledigt? Schreibe Sätze.

- done his homework ✓
- tidied his room
- gone to the supermarket to get some crisps ✓
- put some muffins in his bag ✓

Jason has already ______________________________

He has already ______________________________

He has already ______________________________

7 Sorry, I can't!

Talk to a partner. Sprecht zu zweit.

Would you like to go skateboarding with me?

Sorry, I can't! I haven't tidied my room yet.

go skateboarding | watch a film | go to the cinema | play football | go riding | play video games | eat a pizza | ...

tidied my room | done my homework | eaten dinner | fed my pet | emptied the dishwasher | helped my parents | ...

8 What has changed?

a) **Look at the pictures of the party room. Find the differences.**
Sieh dir die Bilder des Partyraumes an. Finde die Unterschiede.

In picture 1 there ...

In picture 2 there ...

are kids – are no kids | is party punch – is no party punch | is a cat – is no cat | are balloons in the air – are balloons on the floor | ...

1

2

b) Read the sentences. Then look at picture 2 again. Tick true or false.
Lies die Sätze. Dann sieh dir Bild 2 erneut an. Mache ein Häkchen bei richtig oder falsch.

	true	false
1. The kids have left the room.	☐	☐
2. They have drunk the party punch.	☐	☐
3. They have closed the windows.	☐	☐
4. They have eaten all the sausages.	☐	☐
5. They have taken down the balloons.	☐	☐
6. They have cleaned the room.	☐	☐
7. Someone has forgotten his/her rucksack.	☐	☐
8. Someone has left a costume.	☐	☐

9 Have you ever ...?

a) Lies die Fragen in b) unten. Wie heißen sie auf Deutsch? Sprecht zu zweit.

1. Bist du schon einmal auf einer Halloween-Party gewesen?

2. Hast du schon einmal ...?

b) Ask your classmates. Befrage deine Klassenkameraden.

question	name	yes	no
1. Have you ever been to a Halloween party?			
2. Have you ever worn a costume?			
3. Have you ever carved a pumpkin?			
4. Have you ever met a film star?			
5. Have you ever been to London?			

Theme 2

What's on near you?

In diesem *Theme* beschäftigst du dich mit …

- dem Leben in der Stadt und auf dem Land,
- Veranstaltungen in deinem Wohnort,
- Wikingern in England,
- dem Jorvik Viking Festival.

1 Different places

a) Look at picture A. Talk to a partner. Say what you see.
Sieh dir Bild A an. Sprecht zu zweit. Sagt, was ihr seht.

At the top I can see …

I can see …

b) Listen and point. 10
Höre zu und zeige.

c) Look at picture B and make sentences. Draw lines.
Sieh dir Bild B an und bilde Sätze. Verbinde.

1. A man	is riding his bike.
2. A boy	is skateboarding.
3. A boy with a blue cap	are playing football in the park.
4. A woman	is washing his car.
5. Two teenagers	is walking her dog.

2 Where you live

a) Match the words and the pictures. Number. There is one word left.
Ordne die Wörter den Bildern zu. Nummeriere. Ein Wort bleibt übrig.

1

2

3

4

5

6

7

8

9

☐ bus stop	☐ cinema	☐ playground	☐ shopping centre
☐ park	☐ station	☐ library	☐ swimming pool
☐ shop	1 sports club		

b) What is there in your city or village?
Was gibt es in deiner Stadt oder deinem Dorf?

There is a park in my village.

There are two cinemas in my city.

3 A blog

a) Read the blog entries. Underline where the children live.
Lies die Blogeinträge. Unterstreiche, wo die Kinder leben.

Sally

Last weekend I went to London.

There are great sights and shops and restaurants.

I'm happy to be back home in my little town.

What about you guys? Are you happy where you live?

Jamie

I live in a small town, too.

We've got a youth club. I often go there with my friends.

There's also a big park and a lake.

But I'd like to have some good shops and a cinema.

Myra

I'm a city girl.

There's so much to see and do in a city.

And there are people from so many different cultures here. I like that.

b) Read the blog entries again. Tick true or false.
Lies die Blogeinträge erneut. Mache ein Häkchen bei richtig oder falsch.

	true	false
1. Sally went to London last weekend.	☐	☐
2. She lives in London.	☐	☐
3. In Jamie's town there are lots of shops and a cinema.	☐	☐
4. Myra lives in a city.	☐	☐
5. There are lots of people from different cultures.	☐	☐

7 A chat

a) Listen and read along. Höre zu und lies mit. 11

Hi Megan, are you free this weekend?

Yes, any plans?

We could go to the cinema or a concert.

Yeah, cool. But I've already spent most of my pocket money.

What about the Science Museum?

I went there last weekend with my dad.

OK. Let me think …

There's a car boot sale on Sunday. You can buy cool things and everything is cheap.

Sounds good. 👍

And later we can have cake and hot chocolate at my grandma's house.

😋

b) Read the chat again. What ideas do the girls have?
Lies den Chat erneut. Welche Ideen haben die Mädchen?

cinema, ______________________________

____

8 A poster

Sieh dir das Poster an. Berichte jemandem, der kein Englisch kann.

Der Flohmarkt findet jeden ersten ________________ von April bis ________________ statt.

Er startet um ________ Uhr.

Für Verkäufer mit Auto kostet es ____________.

Man kann zum Beispiel ________________ und ________________ kaufen.

Car Boot Sale
1st Sunday of each month
(April – October)

Opening hours:
Open from 10 a.m. – 4 p.m.

cars: £10 vans: £20
Free entry for buyers

Old and new items can be sold: clothes, books, games, toys, and more

Snacks, cakes and drinks available

For further information please call
07623 860522

10 I'll take it

Listen to the dialogue. What does the girl buy? Circle. 12
Höre dir den Dialog an. Was kauft das Mädchen? Kreise ein.

11 At the car boot sale

a) Look at the pictures. What are Megan and Jasmine doing? Tick.
Sieh dir die Bilder an. Was machen Megan und Jasmine? Mache ein Häkchen.

They are buying things at the car boot sale. ☐	They are meeting friends at the car boot sale. ☐

b) Listen and read along. Höre zu und lies mit. 13

On Sunday Megan and Jasmine went to the car boot sale. There were lots of stalls. Megan only had five pounds.
They came to a stall where a young man was selling phone cases.

Jasmine: Let's have a look here. Wow, these phone cases are great. And they're only £2.50 each.

Megan: Yeah! What do you think about this one? I like the heart on it.

Jasmine: Good choice! I think I'll take the green one with the grey stars.

Seller: Hello girls! I've got a special offer for you today. Two phone cases for £4.

Megan: That's great, thank you! Here you are.

Seller: Thanks. Here's your change.

Jasmine: And here's £2 from me.

Seller: Thanks a lot. Bye.

Megan and Jasmine: Thanks. And have a nice day.

c) Answer the questions. Draw lines. Beantworte die Fragen. Verbinde.

1. Where were Megan and Jasmine?	£2.50.
2. What did a young man sell?	At the car boot sale.
3. What was the price for one?	Two phone cases for £4.
4. What was the special offer?	Phone cases.

12 Buying and selling

a) **Listen to the dialogue and read along.** 14
Höre dir den Dialog an und lies mit.

Hello. Can I help you?

Yes, please. I'd like to have a look at the basketball over there.

Sure. Here you are.

Thanks. How much is it?

Let's say £6.

Good. I'll take it. Here's £10.

Thank you. And here's your change.

Thank you. Bye.

Bye. Have a nice day.

Setze eigene Wörter für die blauen Wörter ein.

b) **Make up your own dialogue.** Mache deinen eigenen Dialog.

13 Target task: Your event booklet

a) **What interesting events are there for young people in your area? Work with a partner and collect ideas.** Welche interessanten Veranstaltungen für junge Leute gibt es in deiner Gegend? Arbeitet zu zweit und sammelt Ideen.

flea market | Christmas market | music festival | concert | Easter fire | street festival | open-air cinema | ...

b) **Complete the table with your ideas.** Ergänzt die Tabelle mit euren Ideen.

event	when?	where?	more information
Christmas market	December	school	Christmas play

1 Vikings

a) Look at the picture. Talk to a partner. Say what you see.
Sieh dir das Bild an. Sprecht zu zweit. Sagt, was ihr seht.

I can see ...

Ihr könnt euch auch auf Deutsch austauschen.

b) What do you know about the Vikings? Was wisst ihr über die Wikinger?

2 The Jorvik Viking Festival

a) Listen and read along. Höre zu und lies mit. 15

Date	Time	Place	Event	
15th – 23rd February	10 a.m. – 4 p.m.	St Sampson's Square Stage	**Have a Go Sword** Learn how to fight like a Viking.	
22nd February	11 a.m.	St Sampson's Square Stage	**Strongest Viking Competition** Find out when the strongest Vikings fight against each other.	
22nd February	3 p.m.	St Sampson's Square Stage	**Best Beard Competition** Who has the best beard in the country? Men, women and children can take part.	

b) Berichte jemandem über das Festival, der kein Englisch versteht. (Tag, Zeit, Ort, Was passiert dort?)

3 A day at the festival

a) Look at the picture. Say what you see. Sieh dir das Bild an. Sag, was du siehst.

b) Then listen and read along. Dann höre zu und lies mit. 16

Part 1

It is Saturday morning.

Ben, Sarah and their dad are at the Jorvik Viking Festival in York.

They are at the front of the stage to watch the Strongest Viking Competition.

Afterwards Ben, Sarah and their dad go to the stalls.

There are lots of people with Viking costumes.

Sarah asks a woman with a beautiful costume for a selfie.

Then Sarah asks Ben to give her a bag. It's on the back of her wheelchair.

"We have to go back to the stage now," says Sarah.

"But why?" asks Ben.

"Please, Ben, we have to go now," answers Sarah. "It's something exciting ..."

c) Read the questions. Find the answers in the text. Look at the box for help. Lies die Fragen. Finde die Antworten im Text. Du findest Hilfe im Kasten unten.

1. What day is it? ______
2. Where are Ben and Sarah? ______
3. What does Sarah ask for? ______
4. What does she want to have? ______
5. Where does she want to go? ______

a selfie | Jorvik Viking Festival | a bag | Saturday | to the stage

d) Listen to the second part of the story and read along. 17
Höre dir den zweiten Teil der Geschichte an und lies mit.

Part 2

So Ben, Sarah and their dad go back to the stage.

Ben is surprised to see lots of people with big beards.

There are even women and children with beards. But they aren't real ones.

Sarah opens her bag and takes out a big beard.

"What is that?" asks Ben.

"A beard, of course! I'm taking part in the Best Beard Competition!" answers Sarah.

Ben and his dad look at Sarah in surprise.

Then the competition starts. Men, women and children show off their beards.

Sarah's beard is very long and colourful.

Sarah wins the competition and gets the Best Beard trophy.

e) Read again. Then find the correct ending. Draw lines.
Lies den Text erneut. Dann finde das richtige Ende. Verbinde.

1. Ben sees lots of people	Best Beard Competition.
2. There are women and children	long and colourful.
3. Sarah takes part in the	with big beards.
4. Sarah's beard is	the competition.
5. She wins	with beards.

4 What happened?

a) Read the second part of the story again.
Lies noch einmal den zweiten Teil der Geschichte.

b) Find these sentences in the story. Underline. Then copy the sentences.
Finde diese Sätze in der Geschichte. Unterstreiche sie. Dann schreibe sie ab.

1. Aber das sind keine echten (Bärte).

____

2. Ben und sein Vater schauen Sarah erstaunt an.

____

3. Sarahs Bart ist sehr lang und farbenfroh.

____

5 What is it?

Match the words and the pictures. Number.
Ordne die Wörter den Bildern zu. Nummeriere.

1

2

3

4

5

6

☐ stall ☐ beard ☐ costume

☐ trophy ☐ stage ☐ wheelchair

8 Festival pictures

a) Look at the pictures. Say what you see.
Sieh dir die Bilder an. Sag, was du siehst.

1

2

3

4

5

b) Read the sentences. Match them with the pictures. Number.
Lies die Sätze. Ordne sie den Bildern zu. Nummeriere.

- [ ] This is the beard which Sarah and her mum made.
- [ ] Lizzy is the woman who took a selfie with Sarah.
- [ ] These are the people who took part in the Strongest Viking Competition.
- [1] Sarah is the girl who took part in the Best Beard Competition.
- [ ] This is the trophy which Sarah won.

9 A phone call

a) Listen and repeat. Höre zu und sprich nach. 18

helmet

shield

sword

axe

cape

b) Listen to the phone call. Who is talking? Tick. 19
Höre dir das Telefongespräch an. Wer spricht? Mache Häkchen.

 ☐  ☐  ☐

c) Look at the pictures. Then listen again. Circle the correct costume.
Sieh dir die Bilder an. Dann höre erneut zu. Kreise das richtige Kostüm ein.

10 Choose an activity

- **Complete the words.** Vervollständige die Wörter.

1. c _ m p _ t _ t _ _ n
2. c _ s t _ m _
3. s w _ r d
4. s h _ _ l d
5. b _ _ r d

- **Number the things in the picture.**
Nummeriere die Gegenstände im Bild.

1. helmet
2. shield
3. sword
4. beard
5. cape

11 The grand finale of the festival

a) **What was happening during the grand finale of the Jorvik Viking Festival? Match the sentences and the pictures. Number.**
Was passierte während des großen Finales beim Jorvik Wikinger Festival? Ordne die Sätze den Bildern zu. Nummeriere.

1

2

3

4

5

- [ ] Mr Hancock was wearing Sarah's beard.
- [ ] Ben and Sarah were taking lots of photos.
- [ ] Lots of people were enjoying the beautiful fireworks.
- [ ] The visitors were watching the battle.
- [ ] Ben was holding a torch.

b) **What happened when? Look at the pictures again. Then write sentences.**
Was ist wann passiert? Sieh dir die Bilder erneut an. Dann schreibe Sätze.

1. At 6:45 Ben was ____________________
2. At 7:00 Mr Hancock ____________________
3. At 9:00 ____________________

____

14 Target task: Your festival costume

a) Design your costume for the Jorvik Viking Festival or another festival.
Entwirf dein Kostüm für das Jorvik Wikinger Festival oder ein anderes Fest.

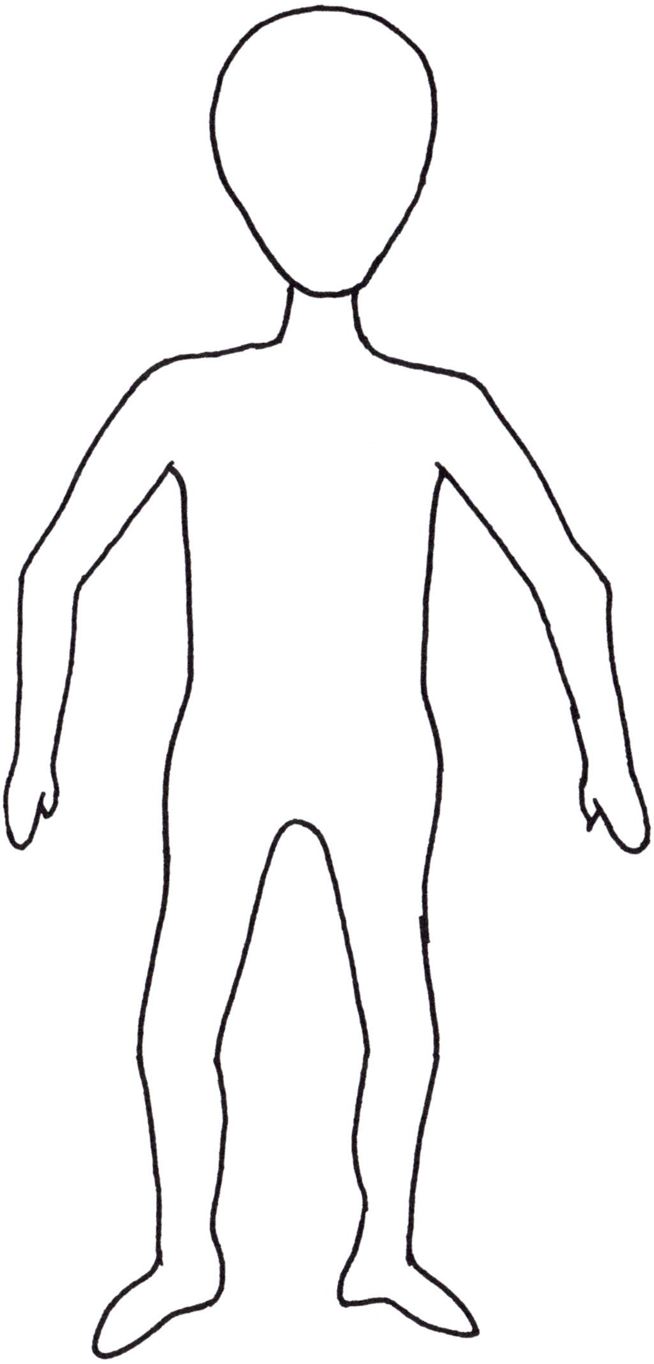

b) Look up words you don't know and label your costume.
Schlage unbekannte Wörter nach und beschrifte dein Kostüm.

c) Present your costume in class.
Präsentiere dein Kostüm in der Klasse.

Theme 3

You're not alone

In diesem *Theme* beschäftigst du dich mit ...

- der Geschichte von Robinson Crusoe,
- persönlichen Problemen,
- Problemlösungen,
- deinem Lieblingslied.

1 Alone on an island

Look at the picture. Talk about it with a partner.
Sieh dir das Bild an. Sprecht zu zweit darüber.

I can see	an island.
There is	palm trees.
There are	a beach.
It's	a (message in a) bottle.
	beautiful.
	no one.

a rope

an axe

soap

a bottle

sunglasses

a book

a knife

a spade

matches

a toothbrush

?
...

2 Your survival kit

a) **Listen and repeat.** Höre zu und sprich nach. 20

b) **Look at the photos. Circle 5 things that you would take on a desert island.** Sieh dir die Fotos an. Kreise 5 Dinge ein, die du auf eine einsame Insel mitnehmen würdest.

c) **What do you need your 5 things for on a desert island?** Wozu brauchst du deine 5 Dinge auf einer einsamen Insel?

I need a bottle to collect rainwater.

I need __________

I need __________

I need __________

I need __________

to start a fire | to clean my teeth | to build a house | to collect rainwater | to catch wild animals | ...

3 Robinson Crusoe

a) Read the story of Robinson Crusoe.
Lies die Geschichte über Robinson Crusoe.

1

In 1659 Robinson left England on a ship to the Caribbean.

2

The ship crossed the Atlantic Ocean.

3

There was a storm and the ship hit some rocks.

4

Robinson swam to an island.

5

He began a new life on the island. He lived alone for many years.

6 

Robinson rescued a man from a group of cannibals. He gave him the name Friday.

7 

Robinson taught Friday to speak English.

8 

Friday taught Robinson how to fish.

9 

In December 1686 an English ship rescued them.

10 

In June 1687 Robinson and Friday arrived in England.

b) Read the story with a partner. Make it sound exciting.
Lest die Geschichte zu zweit. Lasst sie spannend klingen.

4 How did he feel?

a) **Match the words. Draw lines.**
Ordne die Wörter einander zu. Verbinde.

surprised	aufgeregt
excited	froh
glad	überrascht

sad	hilflos
lonely	krank vor Heimweh
homesick	traurig
worried	verängstigt
helpless	besorgt
scared	einsam

b) **Look at pages 46–47 again.**
How did Robinson feel? Talk to a partner.
Sieh dir die Seiten 46–47 erneut an.
Wie fühlte sich Robinson? Sprecht zu zweit.

I think Robinson felt excited in picture number 2.

5 Working with words

Find your way through the maze. You can only step on words that have to do with Robinson Crusoe.
Finde deinen Weg durch das Labyrinth. Du kannst nur auf Wörtern vorankommen, die mit Robinson Crusoe zu tun haben.

Start →	ship	car boot sale	shorts	school
cow	storm	dog	playground	table
earrings	rocks	island	sunglasses	girl
cape	helmet	alone	cannibals	Friday
pencil	farm	shoes	money	rescue
sunshine	bird	pizza	elephant	**End**

9 I'd like to know ...

a) Listen to the people. Where are they? Circle. 21
Höre den Leuten zu. Wo sind sie? Kreise ein.

b) How many of the people would like to live on a desert island? Circle.
Wie viele der Leute würden gern auf einer einsamen Insel leben? Kreise ein.

2 | 11 | 18

c) Listen to the second part. Number the questions. 22
Höre dir den zweiten Teil an. Nummeriere die Fragen.

- [ ] What did you miss most?
- [ ] How did you brush your teeth?
- [1] What did you like about the island?
- [ ] What did you hate about the island?
- [ ] How did you fish?

d) Find the matching answers. Number.
Finde die passenden Antworten. Nummeriere.

- [ ] I liked the beach and the water.
- [ ] I hated the cannibals.
- [ ] I used a stick and water.
- [ ] I missed my family most.
- [ ] I used a stick for fishing.

12 A message in a bottle

Du und dein kleiner Bruder finden diese Flaschenpost. Dein kleiner Bruder versteht nur wenig Englisch. Beantworte seine Fragen.

1. Von wem ist die Flaschenpost?
2. Warum hat das Mädchen sie geschrieben?
3. Was sollen wir als Finder jetzt tun?

91 Camden High Street
London

Dear finder,

My name is Rosie Miller.

I am in year 9 at Haverstock School in London, England.

I am writing this message in a bottle because we are talking about Robinson Crusoe at school.

Please write to me.

Best wishes,

Rosie Miller

14 Target task: Your dream island

a) Listen to Sandeep talking about his dream island. Tick the correct pictures.
Höre Sandeep zu, der über seine Trauminsel spricht. Mache ein Häkchen an die richtigen Bilder. 23 ✓

beach

mountains

hut

rocks

palm trees

river

lake

wild animals

b) Draw a picture of your dream island and label it.
Zeichne ein Bild deiner Trauminsel und beschrifte sie.

Benutze die Wörter von a) oder schaue im Wörterbuch nach.

c) Now write about your dream island. Nun schreibe über deine Trauminsel.

There is ...

There are ...

On my dream island there is ____________________

____

____

____

____

d) Present your dream island to the class.
Präsentiere deine Trauminsel in der Klasse.

1 Letters to Holly

a) Read the letters. Then match the headings and the letters.
Lies die Briefe. Dann ordne die Überschriften den Briefen zu.

☐ Mum's boyfriend

☐ I want a girlfriend

1 The problem is I'm not as good-looking or funny as my classmates.
So the girls at school just ignore me.
I'm really frustrated.
I would like to have a girlfriend but I don't know how to get one.
What can I do?
Henry, 14

Du kannst dir die Briefe auch anhören. 24

2 I really need your help.
My mother has a new boyfriend.
His name is Brian.
Brian will soon move into our house and live with us.
I don't like that idea at all.
I'm worried that Brian will tell me what to do.
Ayla, 13

b) Read the letters again and underline the correct answer.
Lies die Briefe erneut und unterstreiche die richtige Antwort.

1. Henry doesn't think	**he is good-looking**	**he is clever** .
2. He wants to have	**a new mobile phone**	**a girlfriend** .
3. Ayla's problem is	**her mum's new boyfriend**	**school** .
4. Brian will	**marry Ayla's mum**	**move into their house** .

c) **Read Holly's answers. Underline the advice you like best.**
Lies Hollys Antworten. Unterstreiche die Ratschläge, die du am besten findest.

Du kannst dir Hollys Antworten auch anhören. 25

1 Dear Henry,
Don't worry too much, just try to talk to a girl you like.
My advice is to stay cool and smile at her.
If she likes you too, then spend time together.
Ask her to go to the cinema or the park.

2 Dear Ayla,
You should talk to your mum about how you feel.
Tell her about your worries.
Give Brian a chance.
Watch films together and do other fun activities to get to know each other better.

d) **Sprecht zu zweit und auf Deutsch über die Ratschläge. Wie findet ihr sie? Sind sie hilfreich oder eher weniger hilfreich?**

2 Who is it?

Read the letters on page 52 again. Then match the sentence parts.
Lies die Briefe auf Seite 52 erneut. Dann verbinde die Satzteile.

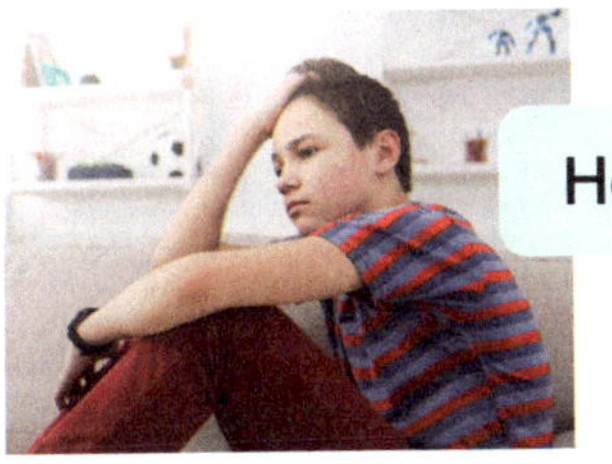
Henry

Ayla

is really frustrated.

worries that everything will be different soon.

doesn't think he is good-looking.

has a mum with a boyfriend.

6 Holly's advice

a) Read Logan's letter. Lies Logans Brief.

There are so many things I want to buy, for example a new computer.
I get pocket money once a month but I always spend it very quickly.
I often have to borrow money from my brother and friends.
I don't know what to do. Please help me.
Logan, 14

b) What is Logan's problem? Underline the correct answer.
Was ist Logans Problem? Unterstreiche die richtige Antwort.

Logan wants to buy a new	**bike**	**computer** .
He spends his pocket money very	**quickly**	**slowly** .
He borrows money from	**his father**	**his friends** .

c) Here are some of Holly's possible answers. Match the sentence parts.
Hier sind einige mögliche Antworten von Holly. Verbinde die Satzteile.

Talk about it	you buy.
Get a job	with your parents.
Think before	what you spend your money on.
You could write down	to earn some money.

d) Write an answer to Logan. Choose some advice from c).
Schreibe eine Antwort an Logan. Wähle Ratschläge aus c) aus.

Dear Logan,
You should talk ____________________
Think ____________________
You could ____________________
____

7 Sandeep and his family

a) Look at the pictures. Who are the people?
Sieh dir die Bilder an. Wer sind die Leute?

b) Read about Sandeep's family.
Lies über Sandeeps Familie.

Du kannst dir die Texte auch anhören. 26

Sandeep's father, Mr Chopra, has got a shop with his wife.
Three months ago a new supermarket opened up around the corner. Many people do their shopping there now.
It's hard for Mr Chopra because he doesn't earn enough money.

Sandeep's mother, Mrs Chopra, has got a shop with her husband.
She likes working in the shop. But she would also like to spend more time with her children.
She and her husband argue a lot.

Sandeep's sister, Neela, is 8.
She is normally a happy girl. But these days Neela is sad because her parents argue a lot.
Then she goes to her room and worries about the future.
Will her mum or dad leave the family?

Sandeep's brother, Pradeep, is 10.
He hates it when his parents argue.
He doesn't want to do his homework or talk about his problems.
He just sits in his room and plays video games.

Sandeep is 13.
He often helps his parents in their shop.
He worries that his parents will have to close down the shop.
He cheers himself up by playing the guitar and thinking about Jasmine.

8 The family members

Read the facts. Then match them with the family members. Draw lines.
Lies die Fakten. Dann ordne sie den Familienmitgliedern zu. Verbinde.

Mrs Chopra — Mr Chopra — Neela — Pradeep — Sandeep

8; normally a happy girl; worries about the future; fears that mum or dad will leave the family	has got a shop; new supermarket around the corner; shop is losing money	13; helps in the shop; worries that parents will have to close down the shop; cheers himself up with music	has got a shop; would like to spend more time with her children; argues with her husband	10; hates it when his parents argue; doesn't talk about his problems; plays video games

10 Talking to a friend

Listen to Megan and Sandeep. Put the pictures in the right order. 27
Höre Megan und Sandeep zu. Bringe die Bilder in die richtige Reihenfolge.

12 On Sunday

a) **What will the Chopras do on Sunday? Match the sentences and the pictures.**
Was werden die Chopras am Sonntag machen? Ordne die Sätze den Bildern zu.

1. If the weather is bad, Sandeep will play video games.
2. If the Chopras can agree on a good film, they will watch it together.
3. If Mr Chopra doesn't have to work in the shop, he will make a delicious curry.
4. If Neela feels good, she will put on a sari.
5. If Mrs Chopra has enough time, she will read a book.
6. If the weather is nice, Sandeep will go skateboarding.

b) **What will you do on Sunday? Complete the sentences.**
Was wirst du am Sonntag machen? Vervollständige die Sätze.

1. If I have enough time, I will ______________________________
2. If the weather is nice, I will ______________________________
3. If the weather is bad, I will ______________________________
4. If I feel good, I will ______________________________

ride my bike | read a book | watch a film | meet my friends | go swimming | relax on the sofa | tidy my room | listen to music | chat with ... | sing | ...

13 Don't worry, be happy

When Sandeep is unhappy, he likes listening to music.

a) **Listen to one of Sandeep's favourite songs. Circle the words you hear.** Höre dir eines von Sandeeps Lieblingsliedern an. Kreise die Wörter ein, die du verstanden hast.

song | wrote | note | worry | happy | life | trouble | double | now

b) **Listen again and read along.** Höre erneut zu und lies mit.

Here's a little song I wrote.
You might want to sing it note for note.
Don't worry, be happy.
In every life we have some trouble.
But when you worry, you make it double.
Don't worry, be happy.
Don't worry, be happy now.

Don't worry, be happy. Don't worry, be happy.
Don't worry, be happy. Don't worry, be happy.

c) **Sprecht zu zweit und auf Deutsch über den Song. Worum geht es in ihm?**

14 Your favourite music

Write about your favourite song. Schreibe über dein Lieblingslied.

My favourite song is ______
The singer is ______
The style is ______
I like ______
I can understand some of the words: ______

the style: pop, rock, electronic, hip hop, techno, country, heavy metal, ...

I like: the melody, the lyrics, the rhythm, the voice of the singer, ...

15 How to deal with problems

What can you do when you have a problem? Match the sentence parts.
Was kannst du machen, wenn du ein Problem hast? Verbinde die Satzteile.

You can talk to	a helpline.
You can chat	friends or parents.
You can call	sports.
You can do	your diary.
You can write an	with friends.
You can write in	email to an agony aunt.

16 Target task: Give a helping hand

a) **Look at the photo. What could be the problem?**
Sieh dir das Foto an. Was könnte das Problem sein?

b) **Work with a partner. Put the speech bubbles in the right order.**
Arbeitet zu zweit. Bringt die Sprechblasen in die richtige Reihenfolge.

- What's wrong? 1
- Oh no!
- Ask my brother. He is good at English. He can help you.
- She never listens to me.
- Good idea.
- Why don't you talk to your mum first?
- My dad will be really angry.
- I got a bad mark in the English test.

c) **Listen and check. Then read out the dialogue with a partner.** 28
Höre zu und vergleiche. Dann lest den Dialog zu zweit.

Theme 4

Everyday science

In diesem *Theme* beschäftigst du dich mit ...

- früheren Formen der Kommunikation,
- Handys und ähnlichen Geräten,
- Erfindungen,
- einem Museum in England.

B

A

C

D

1 A very short history of communication

a) Look at the pictures. Say what you see.
Sieh dir die Bilder an. Sag, was du siehst.

In picture A I can see ...

Ihr könnt euch bei a) auch auf Deutsch austauschen. Bei b) müsst ihr nicht jedes Wort verstehen. Achtet auf Keywords (Schlüsselwörter).

b) Listen and read along. Then match the texts with the pictures. 29
Höre zu und lies mit. Dann ordne die Texte den Bildern zu.

☐ About 5,000 years ago people in Egypt wrote their **signs on papyrus**.

☐ In 1876 Alexander Graham Bell invented the **telephone**.

E

F

G

H

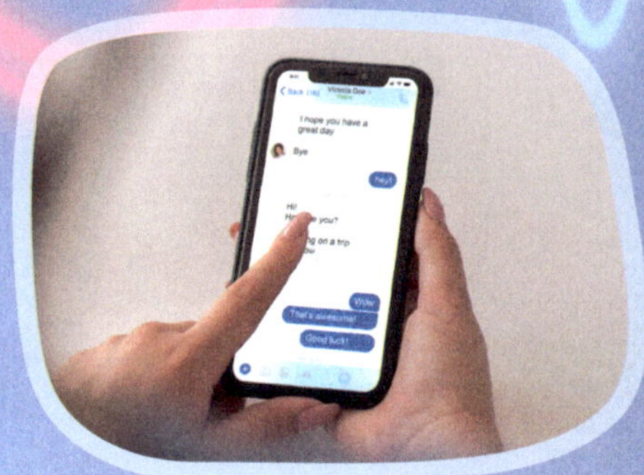

☐ In the Stone Age people lived together in **caves**. They painted pictures on the cave walls and made sounds and **signs with their hands**.

☐ People used **smoke signals**, flags or mirrors to send messages.

☐ Now **computers** are everywhere. We can use the Internet to get information from all over the world and **send emails** in seconds.

☐ 600 years ago people in Europe started to **write letters** on real paper.

☐ People could buy the first **smartphones** in 2007.

☐ The **first computers** in the 20th century were **as big as a room**.

4 Computers & Co.

a) What can you do with a computer or mobile phone? Label the pictures.
Was kannst du mit einem Computer oder Handy machen? Beschrifte die Bilder.

download/listen to music | search for information | phone people | write a text message | take photos/selfies | send emails

1

2

3

4

5

6

b) Talk to a partner. Sprecht zu zweit.

Have you got a computer or a mobile phone?

Yes, I have got a computer.

No, I haven't got a computer.

What do you do with the computer?

I send emails.

5 A new experience

a) **Imagine you <u>can't</u> use your computer or mobile phone for a week. Underline your answers. Then talk to a partner.**
Stell dir vor, du kannst deinen Computer oder dein Handy eine Woche lang nicht benutzen. Unterstreiche deine Antworten. Dann sprecht zu zweit.

How would you feel?	What would you do instead?
I would feel ... sad / unhappy / frustrated lonely / bored / happy ...	I think I would ... meet friends | watch films | listen to music | do homework | go to the cinema | do sports | visit my grandparents | read a book | ...

b) **Listen to the teenagers. Underline the correct information.** 30
Höre den Teenagern zu. Unterstreiche die richtigen Informationen.

	Kezia 	**Andy** 
Why couldn't they use their mobile phones?	phone fell into the toilet / phone fell into a lake	parents took it away / lost it on the bus
What did they do instead?	listened to music / started reading books	studied hard and went to the park / went skating and phoned friends
How did they feel during that time?	angry / happy	frustrated and good / aggressive and unhappy

c) **Listen again and check.** Höre erneut zu und vergleiche.

6 Sharing information

a) Listen to the first part of the story and read along. 31
Höre dir den ersten Teil der Geschichte an und lies mit.

It was a Sunday evening and Jasmine was in her room.
It was late and Jasmine was tired, but she always posted a video on Sunday evening.

With a little bit of make-up Jasmine felt better and started taking some selfies.
Then she filmed her video and told her friends and followers about her weekend.
At the end she said: "I'm sorry, guys. I'm not happy with myself and how I look today. But I hope you enjoyed my video. Bye!"
Afterwards she uploaded the video and got ready for bed.

Jasmine loved reading the comments and seeing the likes, but there was no reaction from Megan.

In the morning Jasmine was still tired. When she checked her phone, her video had hundreds of likes and lots of comments.
But there was still no reaction from Megan.

At school Jasmine walked over to Megan to talk to her.

b) Tick the correct sentence. Mache ein Häkchen an den richtigen Satz.

- [ ] Jasmine is tired because she filmed a video and posted it.
- [ ] Jasmine is tired because she watched a lot of films.

c) **Now listen to the second part of the story and read along.** 32
Nun höre dir den zweiten Teil der Geschichte an und lies mit.

Megan: I'm sorry I didn't watch your video. I was tired. I don't want to spend so much time online anymore. I want to spend more time doing other things.

Jasmine: OK.

Megan: And I think I'll delete[1] some of my social media accounts.

Jasmine: But why?

Megan: I prefer[2] seeing my friends in person.

Jasmine: But you could at least watch my videos.

Megan: Well, to be honest[3] with you, sometimes I think you share a bit too much. And there are things you just shouldn't share online.

Jasmine: Really? Like what?

Megan: Well, last week, for example, you posted an embarrassing[4] photo of Jason.

Jasmine: That was only a joke! But maybe you're right. I think I should delete that photo.

Megan: It can also be dangerous to share too much information online. You don't know who is reading your posts or watching your videos.

Jasmine: OK, OK, I get it. I'll try to be a bit more careful.

1 delete: *löschen*; 2 prefer: *lieber mögen*; 3 honest: *ehrlich*; 4 embarrassing: *peinlich*

d) **Read the second part again. Then underline in different colours.**
Lies noch einmal den zweiten Teil. Dann unterstreiche in verschiedenen Farben.

What does Megan want to do?

What is Megan's advice to Jasmine?

8 The video

Complete the story with the correct words.
Vervollständige die Geschichte mit den richtigen Wörtern.

delete | left | filmed | uploaded | post | spend

On Sunday evening Jasmine wanted to ___ ___ s ___ another video for her friends and followers.

First she ___ ___ l ___ ___ ___ the video. Then she ___ ___ ___ o ___ ___ ___ ___ it.

Lots of friends and followers ___ ___ f ___ a comment but Megan didn't.

She doesn't want to ___ ___ ___ ___ d so much time online anymore.

Maybe she'll also ___ ___ l ___ ___ ___ some of her social media accounts.

9 Staying safe online

a) Lies die folgenden Hinweise. Schlage unbekannte Wörter nach.

How to stay safe online

- Don't post any personal information online – like your address or your mobile number.
- Never tell anyone your passwords.
- Never open emails from someone you don't know.
- If someone sends you a mean message, don't answer.
- Don't put pictures or videos online that you wouldn't want your classmates to see.

b) Arbeitet zu zweit. Beantwortet die Fragen auf Deutsch.

1. Was sollte man nicht ins Internet stellen? |
2. Was sollte man niemandem verraten? |
3. Was sollte man nicht öffnen? |
4. Was sollte man tun, wenn man eine gemeine Nachricht erhält? |
5. Was sollte man nicht online stellen?

11 Target task: Your user manual

a) **Work with a partner. What can you tell people who don't know how to use a mobile phone? Make notes.**
Arbeitet zu zweit. Was könnt ihr Leuten erzählen, die nicht wissen, wie man ein Handy benutzt? Macht Notizen.

Bei Aufgabe 4 (S. 62) findest du Hilfe.

What can you do with a mobile phone?

watch videos | chat with friends | buy things | write emails | ...

b) **Now complete the mobile phone and the user manual.**
Nun vervollständige das Handy und das Benutzerhandbuch.

User manual for a mobile phone

What you can do with a mobile phone

phone people

c) **Present your user manual.** Präsentiere dein Benutzerhandbuch.

1 Inventions

a) Listen and point. Höre zu und zeige. 33

stamp

telephone

light bulb

chocolate chip cookies

computer

bike

matches

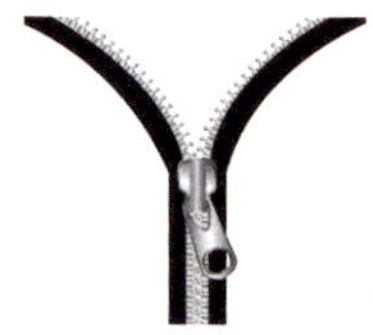

zip

dishwasher

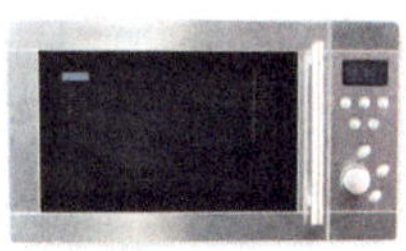

microwave

car

television

b) Talk about the inventions in a) with a partner.
Sprecht zu zweit über die Erfindungen in a).

The bike	is	very important to me.
The computer	are	more important than the car.
Matches		not important to me.
...		

c) What is the most important invention to you? Complete the sentence.
Was ist die wichtigste Erfindung für dich? Vervollständige den Satz.

The ______________________________ is the most important invention to me.

2 Successful inventors

a) Read the information. Then find the correct German sentence. Number.
Lies die Informationen. Dann finde den richtigen deutschen Satz. Nummeriere.

Alexander Graham Bell

Scotland/USA (1876)

His invention is used to talk to people far away. ☐

John Mauchly & John Eckert

USA (1945)

Their invention is used to write, search for information, ... ☐

Thomas Edison

USA (1879)

His invention is used to light rooms and streets. ☐

Josephine Cochrane

USA (1886)

Her invention is used to wash plates, cups, glasses, ... ☐

Karl Benz

Germany (1876)

His invention is used to travel long distances on roads. ☐

Philo Farnsworth

USA (1928)

His invention is used to watch programmes. ☐

1. Seine Erfindung wird genutzt, um Räume und Straßen zu beleuchten.
2. Seine Erfindung wird genutzt, um Sendungen zu schauen.
3. Ihre Erfindung wird genutzt, um Geschirr zu waschen.
4. Seine Erfindung wird genutzt, um mit Leuten zu sprechen.
5. Ihre Erfindung wird genutzt, um zu schreiben, nach Infos zu suchen, ...
6. Seine Erfindung wird genutzt, um weite Strecken zu fahren.

b) Talk to a partner about the inventions. Sprecht zu zweit über die Erfindungen.

light bulb | car | television | dishwasher | telephone | computer

The light bulb was invented by Thomas Edison.
It was invented in 1879.

3 Invented by?

Choose two inventions. Then complete the sentences.
Wähle zwei Erfindungen. Dann vervollständige die Sätze.

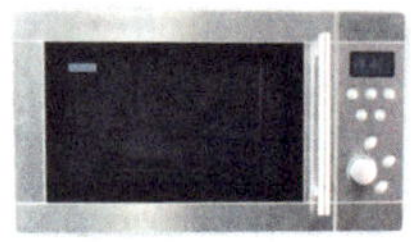

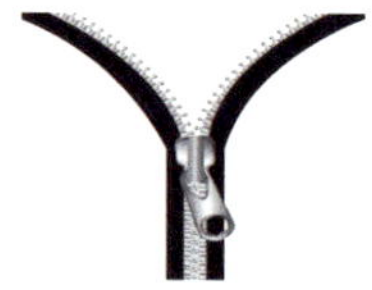

stamp	microwave	bike	zip
James Chalmer	**Percy Spencer**	**Karl Drais**	**Whitcomb Judson**
Scotland (1838)	*the USA (1946)*	*Germany (1817)*	*the USA (1893)*

It was invented by ______________________
It was made in ______________________
It is used to ______________________

It was invented by ______________________
It was made in ______________________
It is used to ______________________

close or open a jacket | send letters | cook food quickly | travel from A to B

5 Odd one out

Circle the odd one out. Kreise das Wort ein, das nicht dazugehört.

1. microwave – dishwasher – car
2. inventor – television – computer
3. computer – zip – matches
4. England – USA – Germany
5. light bulb – car – bike

Vergleicht eure Ergebnisse zu zweit.
Warum habt ihr euch für welches Wort entschieden?
Manchmal gibt es mehrere Möglichkeiten.

6 An invention quiz

What are the inventions? Write them down.
Welche Erfindungen sind es? Schreibe sie auf.

A It is made of paper. It has got a picture and numbers on it. You stick it on a postcard.

B It is made of metal. It has got a door. It needs electricity. It is used to cook food quickly.

C They are made of wood. They have got a red head. They are used to start a fire.

st __ __ __   __ i __ __ __ w __ __ __   m __ t __ __ __ __

8 Emily Cummins

a) **Read the text about Emily.** Lies den Text über Emily.

Emily Cummins was born in 1987. When she was four years old, her grandfather showed her how to make toys from old materials.

When she was 15 years old, she invented a toothpaste dispenser for her other grandfather. It helps people with hand or arm problems to squeeze toothpaste tubes.

Three years later Emily invented a water carrier.
With this carrier African women and children can transport containers of water.

Emily also invented a small fridge that runs without electricity. These solar-powered fridges are used in many African countries.

Emily studied at Leeds University and has won many prizes.

Emily's fridge

b) **What has Emily invented? Tick.** Was hat Emily erfunden? Mache ein Häkchen.

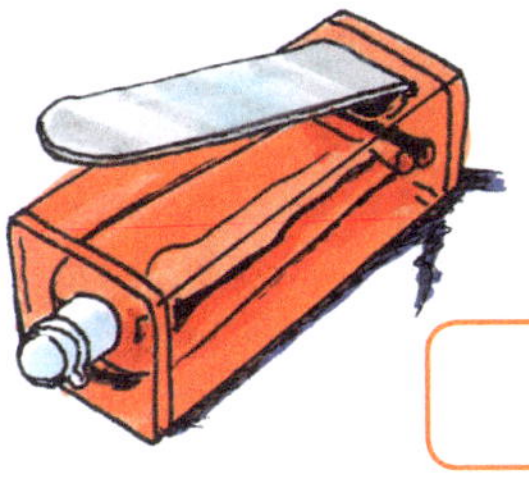 ☐

 ☐

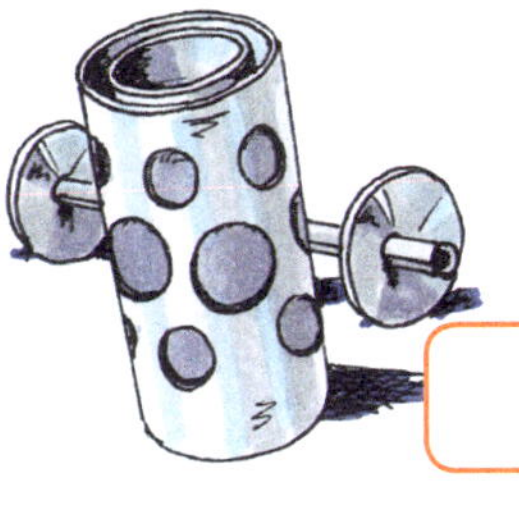 ☐

 ☐

9 The Science and Industry Museum in Manchester

a) **Listen and number the photos.** Höre zu und nummeriere die Fotos. 34

MANCHESTER'S SCIENCE AND INDUSTRY MUSEUM

Find out more about the discoveries and inventions that began in Manchester and changed the world.
Also learn about science and how it works.

Experiment Gallery

☐

Textiles Gallery

☐

Air and Space Hall

☐

Connecting Manchester Gallery

☐

Revolution Manchester Gallery

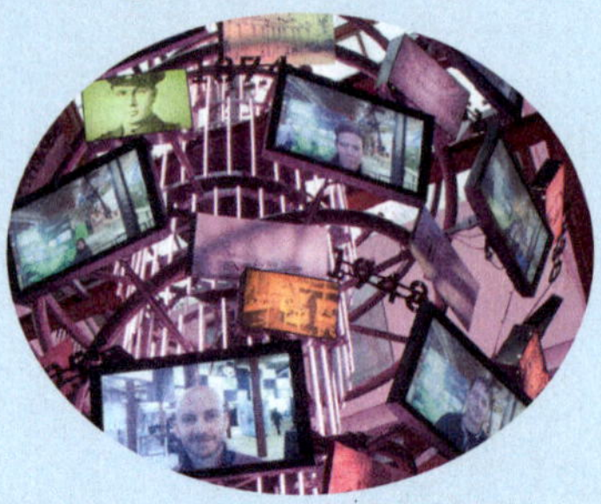

☐

1830 Station

☐

b) Listen again. Then complete the sentences with the correct words.
Höre erneut zu. Dann vervollständige die Sätze mit den richtigen Wörtern.

train station | bike | cars | computers | watch | invented | machines | telephones | ideas

1. See the ___ ___ r ___ , bikes and planes that were ___ ___ v ___ ___ ___ ___ ___ in Manchester, for example an AVRO F monoplane or a Rolls-Royce.
2. Create a tornado, ___ ___ t ___ ___ your own skeleton ride a b ___ ___ ___ or try to lift a Mini.
3. Learn about the cotton-making ___ ___ ___ ___ i ___ ___ ___ .
4. Step into the world's first ___ ___ a ___ ___ ___ t ___ ___ ___ ___ ___ , which is part of the museum.
5. Take a look at early ___ ___ ___ ___ p ___ ___ ___ ___ ___ made in Manchester and meet "Baby", the pioneer for modern ___ ___ ___ ___ u ___ ___ ___ ___ .
6. Find out about Manchester's amazing industrial innovations and scientific i ___ ___ ___ ___ .

c) Where would you like to go? Talk to a partner.
Wo würdest du gern hingehen? Sprecht zu zweit.

I'd like to go to the Experiment Gallery.

The Experiment Gallery sounds interesting.

LAND & LEUTE

Museen in Großbritannien
Es gibt in Großbritannien Museen zu fast jedem Thema: Teekannen, Rasenmäher, Spielzeug, Pferde, …
Das Besondere an den meisten Museen ist, dass man die Dinge ansehen, anfassen und ausprobieren kann. Häufig kommen interaktive Bildschirme zum Einsatz und es werden spannende Führungen angeboten.
Eine weitere Besonderheit ist, dass man in den meisten Museen keinen Eintritt zahlen muss.

Welche Museen gibt es in deiner Umgebung? Was kann man dort sehen und erleben?

11 Life without electricity

a) What needs electricity? Make a list.
Was braucht Strom? Erstelle eine Liste.

Schlage unbekannte Wörter nach oder frage die Lehrkraft.

toaster

toaster

kettle

hairdryer

...

b) Talk to a partner. Sprecht zu zweit.

I need electricity for the computer.

c) Imagine a day without electricity. Talk to a partner.
Stell dir einen Tag ohne Strom vor. Sprecht zu zweit.

Without electricity	I	couldn't	play	clothes.
	we		watch	emails.
	you		listen to	music.
			write	films.
			wash	warm meals.
			download	video games.
			cook	...
			...	

13 Target task: Your invention

a) **What do you want to invent? Draw a picture.**
Was möchtest du erfinden? Zeichne ein Bild.

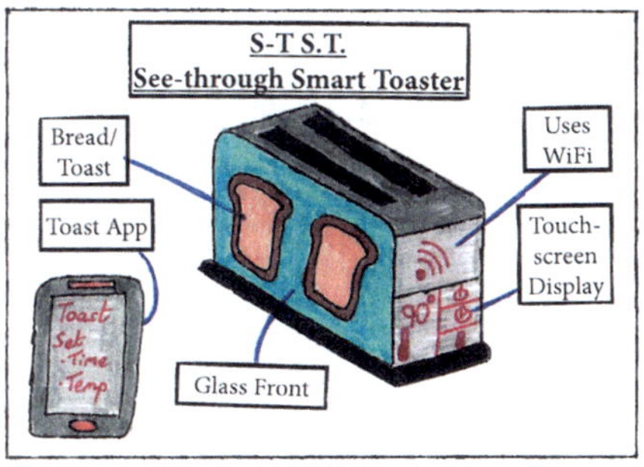

b) **Label the parts of your invention. Look up words you don't know.**
Beschrifte die Teile deiner Erfindung. Schlage unbekannte Wörter nach.

c) **Write about your invention.**
Schreibe über deine Erfindung.

My invention is a smart toaster.
It is used to toast bread.
It is made of metal, plastic and glass.
It has got a touchscreen display and a glass front.

My invention is ______
It is used to ______
It is made of ______
It has got ______

d) **Present your invention in class.** Präsentiere deine Erfindung in der Klasse.

1 England

a) **Colour by numbers.** Male nach Zahlen.

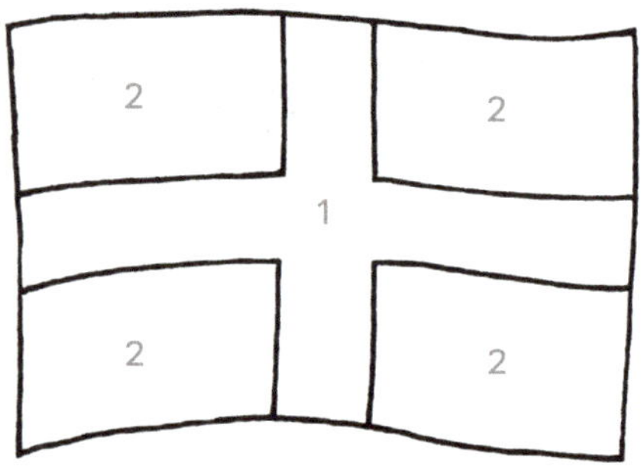

1: red 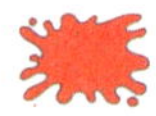

2: white 

b) **Underline the correct information.** Unterstreiche die richtige Information.

England's national animal is the tiger / lion.

England's national flower is the rose / tulip.

England uses the dollar ($) / pound (£).

The main language is German / English.

Hello, how are you?

The capital city is London / Berlin.

c) **Look at the famous sights. Say what you see.**
Sieh dir die berühmten Sehenswürdigkeiten an. Sag, was du siehst.

Stonehenge

Lake District

Windsor Castle

2 Wales

a) Colour by numbers. Male nach Zahlen.

1: red 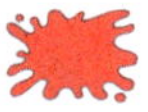

2: green 

3: white 

b) Read the text. Then fill in the words for the pictures.
Lies den Text. Dann trage die Wörter für die Bilder ein.

Wales' national animal is the dragon. 

The capital city is Cardiff. 

The official languages are English and Welsh. Helô!

Wales uses the pound (£). 

The national flower is the daffodil. 

Helô!

c) Berichte jemandem, der kein Englisch versteht, über diese Sehenswürdigkeit.

This is Mount Snowdon.
It is the highest mountain in Wales.
It is 1,085 metres high.

3 Scotland

a) **Colour by numbers.** Male nach Zahlen.

1: blue

2: white

b) **Listen and point.** Höre zu und zeige. 35

unicorn

pound (£)

thistle

Gaelic

Loch Lomond

Ben Nevis

Edinburgh

c) **Read the sentences. Then fill in the words from b).**
Lies die Sätze. Dann füge die Wörter aus b) ein.

1. Scotland's national animal is the __ __ __ c __ __ __ .
2. Scotland's national flower is the __ __ __ s __ l __ .
3. Scotland's capital city is E __ __ __ __ __ __ g __ .
4. Scotland uses the __ o __ __ __ .
5. The main language is English. Some people can speak G __ __ __ __ c.
6. Scotland's highest mountain is __ __ n N __ __ __ __ (1,344 m).
7. The largest lakes are Loch Ness and L __ __ h L __ __ __ __ __ .

4 Northern Ireland

a) Colour by numbers. Male nach Zahlen.

1: red

2: white

b) Match the words with the pictures.
Ordne die Wörter den Bildern zu.

Dia dhuit!

1. pound
2. Irish
3. castle
4. lake
5. shamrock
6. Belfast

c) Read the sentences. Then fill in the words from b).
Lies die Sätze. Dann füge die Wörter aus b) ein.

1. The capital city of Northern Ireland is ___ e ___ f ___ ___ ___ .
2. Northern Ireland uses the ___ o ___ ___ ___ .
3. Northern Ireland's national flower is the s ___ ___ ___ ___ ___ ___ ___ .
4. The main language is English. Another important language is I ___ ___ ___ ___ .
5. Lough Neagh is the largest ___ a ___ ___ in Northern Ireland.
6. A famous ___ ___ ___ t ___ ___ in Northern Ireland is Quintin Castle.

5 Ireland

a) **Colour by numbers.** Male nach Zahlen.

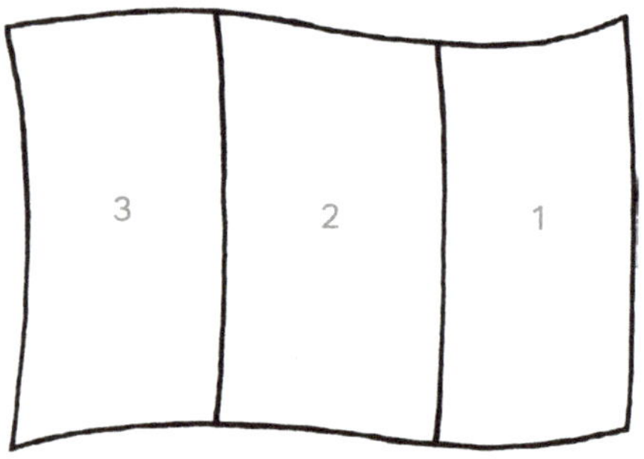

1: orange 

2: white

3: green 

b) **Read the information about Ireland.** Lies die Informationen über Irland.

Capital and largest city:
Dublin (about 554,000 people)
Other large cities include Cork, Limerick and Galway.

Money: Euro (€)

Language: English and Irish are the official languages.

Ireland's national symbol and instrument is the harp.

Ireland's national flower is the shamrock.

c) **Complete the table.** Vervollständige die Tabelle.

capital city	national flower	money	languages

d) **Which of these sights would you like to visit?**
Welche dieser Sehenswürdigkeiten würdest du gerne besichtigen?

Rock of Cashel

Blarney Castle

Kilmainham Gaol

6 Your class trip to the UK and Ireland

a) Plan a class trip to the UK or Ireland. Circle and label.
Plane eine Klassenfahrt in das Vereinigte Königreich oder nach Irland. Kreise ein und beschrifte.

> Schlage unbekannte Wörter nach oder frage die Lehrkraft.

1. We could go to ...

England

2. We could get there by ...

plane

3. We could stay in/at a ...

hotel

4. We could visit a ...

museum

5. We could go ...

hiking

b) Present your plans in class. Präsentiere deine Pläne in der Klasse.

Theme 5

Up and away

In diesem *Theme* beschäftigst du dich mit ...

- Reiseplänen und Ferienaktivitäten,
- dem Fahrkartenkauf an einem Schalter,
- Urlaubszielen in Schottland,
- dem Reservieren von Zimmern.

1 Summer holidays

a) **Listen to the song "Summer Holiday" by Cliff Richard. Circle the words you hear.** Höre dir das Lied „Summer Holiday" von Cliff Richard an. Kreise die Wörter ein, die du verstanden hast.

summer | swimming pool | sea | no more working | holiday | dreams | fun | hotel | sun shines

b) **Do you know other summer words? Collect with a partner.** Kennst du noch andere Sommerwörter? Sammelt zu zweit.

beach,

c) **Talk to a partner.** Sprecht zu zweit.

What would you like to do in the summer holidays?

I'd like to ...

... meet my friends. | ... go swimming. | ... play football. | ... visit my grandma. | ... go to the park. | ...

2 Holidays without parents

a) Look at the picture. Then read and number the sentences.
Sieh dir das Bild an. Dann lies die Sätze und nummeriere sie.

- [ ] There are some children on the bus.
- [ ] The bus driver is putting the bags on the bus.
- [ ] Some children are waiting next to the bus.
- [ ] The parents are waving to their children.
- [ ] A girl is going to the bus.
- [ ] A boy is thinking of having a party on holiday.

b) How do the children feel? Circle and compare with a partner.
Wie fühlen sich die Kinder? Kreise ein und vergleicht zu zweit.

happy | excited | sad | nervous | lonely | ____________

I think they feel ...

3 Making plans

a) Listen to Megan and Ben. What is Megan's idea? Tick. 36
Höre Megan und Ben zu. Welche Idee hat Megan? Mache ein Häkchen.

- [ ] Megan wants to go to Edinburgh with Ben.
- [ ] Megan wants to sleep in, watch films and go cycling.

b) Listen again and read along. Höre erneut zu und lies mit.

Megan:	So what are you going to do in the summer holidays?
Ben:	Well, sleep in, watch films, go cycling ... stuff like that.
Megan:	Are you going anywhere with your family?
Ben:	I don't think so. My dad has to work a lot. And what about you?
Megan:	First I'm going to visit my dad, as usual.
Ben:	Sounds good. Edinburgh is a nice place, isn't it?
Megan:	Yeah, it is. But sometimes it's a bit boring with my dad and his family. Fergus is really cute, but after a while ... I'm just thinking ... Would you like to come to Edinburgh with me ... for a week?
Ben:	Well, I've never been to Edinburgh before.
Megan:	It's not as exciting as London. But there's a great castle and lots of good shops.
Ben:	Cool!

Megan: And we could climb Arthur's Seat. That's an old volcano.

Ben: Wow, I've never heard of it.

Megan: And when it's warm and sunny, we could go to Portobello Beach. It's really nice there.

Ben: A beach? That's great! But where am I going to stay in Edinburgh?

Megan: At my dad's place, of course.

Ben: And how are we going to get to Edinburgh?

Megan: By train. There's a direct one from King's Cross to Edinburgh.

Ben: And how long does it take?

Megan: It takes about five hours. It's faster than going by car. It'll be fun to travel with you.

Ben: You think so?

Megan: Sure. So would you like to come to Edinburgh with me?

Ben: Yeah, sounds like fun. But I have to ask my parents first.

Megan: And I'll phone my dad ...

c) **Now read the dialogue and underline.** Nun lies den Dialog und unterstreiche.

What can you do in Edinburgh?

Where can Megan and Ben stay?

How can they get to Edinburgh?

4 Talking to Dad

a) **Listen to Megan and her dad. Tick the correct answer.** 37
Höre Megan und ihrem Vater zu. Mache ein Häkchen an die richtige Antwort.

- [ ] Megan's dad likes Megan's idea.
- [ ] He doesn't like Ben.

b) **Listen again and underline the correct answer.**
Höre erneut zu und unterstreiche die richtige Antwort.

1. They could show Ben	**castles and Loch Ness**	**beaches and a zoo** .
2. Megan's dad's computer	**is new**	**doesn't work** .
3. Megan is sure Ben will	**like the computer**	**find the problem** .

5 At the station

Megan and Ben are at King's Cross in London.

a) **Look at the map. Then listen and point.** 38
Sieh dir die Karte an. Dann höre zu und zeige.

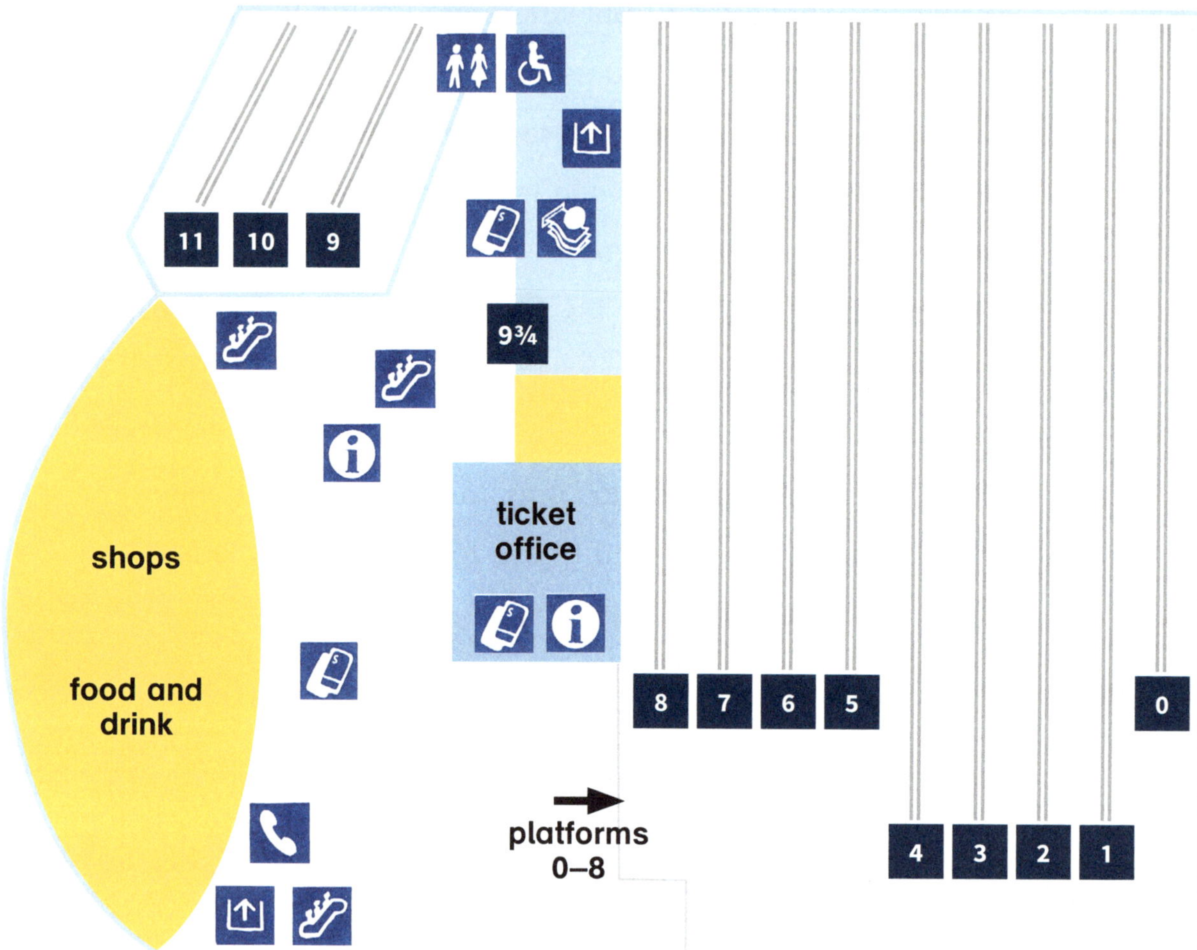

toilets
accessible toilets
escalators
lift
ticket machines
information point
cash machine
telephones

b) **Find the words.** Finde die Wörter.

1. You can buy tickets there: ____________________
2. You can get on the trains there: ____________________
3. You go there when you have a question: ____________________
4. You use it to call someone: ____________________
5. You use it to get money: ____________________
6. You use it to go up or down: ____________________

6 A timetable

Look at the timetable. Then complete the sentences.
Sieh dir den Fahrplan an. Dann vervollständige die Sätze.

Departures

Time	To	Platform
11:30	Edinburgh	1
12:02	Cambridge	11
13:18	Leeds	4

1. The train to Edinburgh leaves at ______________________
2. The train at 13:18 goes to ______________________
3. The train to Cambridge leaves from platform ______________

7 Arrivals and departures

a) **Look at the timetable.** Sieh dir den Fahrplan an.

Departures

Time	To	Platform
10:40	Newcastle	3

Arrivals

Time	From	Platform
13:23	Aberdeen	10

b) **Underline the correct answer.** Unterstreiche die richtige Antwort.

1. The train to Newcastle leaves at **10:40** **13:23** .
2. The train to Newcastle leaves from platform **5** **3** .
3. The train from Aberdeen arrives at platform **3** **10** .

c) **Match the words. Draw lines.** Ordne die Wörter zu. Verbinde.

station | platform | timetable | departure | arrival | ticket office

Bahnsteig | Fahrkartenschalter | Ankunft | Abfahrt | Bahnhof | Fahrplan

8 Station announcements

Höre dir die folgenden Durchsagen an. Beantworte die Fragen von jemandem, der nur wenig Englisch versteht. 39

1. Was ist im Bahnhofsgebäude nicht erlaubt?

____

2. Welcher Zug fällt aus?

____

3. Was ist im Zug erhältlich?

____

Auf einem Bahnhof werden viele Durchsagen gemacht.
Höre genau hin, um wichtige Informationen zu erhalten.

Fahrrad fahren | 17:49 nach Newcastle | Skateboard fahren | Rauchen | kalte und warme Snacks | Rollschuh laufen | 7:49 nach Newcastle

9 At the ticket office

Megan and Ben are at the ticket office.

a) **Listen and read along. Circle the correct words.** 40
Höre zu und lies mit. Kreise die richtigen Wörter ein.

Megan: Two tickets to Edinburgh / London, please.
Man: Single or return?
Megan: Single / Return, please.
Man: OK, that's £156 / £218 altogether.
Megan: Here you are.
Oh, what platform is it, please?
Man: Platform 1 / 2.
Megan: Thank you. And could you tell us when the next train leaves?
Man: You have to hurry.
It leaves in eight / ten minutes.

b) **Read the dialogue with a partner.** Lest den Dialog zu zweit.

11 Helping out

Wie sagst du auf Englisch, dass ...

du eine Rückfahrkarte nach Bristol haben möchtest?	The train leaves at 10:15.
du eine Einzelfahrkarte nach Bristol haben möchtest?	That's £10 altogether.
das zusammen zehn Pfund kostet?	I would like a single ticket to Bristol.
jemand sich beeilen muss?	I would like a return ticket to Bristol.
der Zug auf Gleis 5 ankommt?	You have to hurry.
der Zug um 10:15 abfährt?	The train arrives at platform 5.

12 Target task: Scenes at a station

a) **Work with a partner. Make your own timetable.**
Arbeitet zu zweit. Erstellt euren eigenen Fahrplan.

To	Single / Return	Platform	Departure
	£_______ / £_______		

b) **Now make your own dialogue.** Erstellt jetzt euren eigenen Dialog.

A: Two tickets to ______________________, please.

B: Single or return?

A: ______________________, please.

B: OK, that's £____________ altogether.

A: Here you are. Oh, what platform is it, please?

B: Platform ________.

A: Thank you. And could you tell us when the next train leaves?

B: You have to hurry. It leaves in ________________ minutes.

c) **Act out your dialogue.** Spielt euren Dialog vor.

1 First day in Edinburgh

a) Look at the photos. Then listen and number. 41

Sieh dir die Fotos an. Dann höre zu und nummeriere.

haggis ☐

shops on Princes Street ☐

Edinburgh Castle ☐

bagpiper with kilt ☐

b) Listen again. Circle the correct answers.

Höre erneut zu. Kreise die richtigen Antworten ein.

1. At Edinburgh Castle, Ben looked at Scotland's Crown Jewels / the Queen.
2. The One o'Clock Gun is fired every day at one o'clock / two o'clock.
3. Ben and Megan bought T-shirts / caps.
4. Ben thinks the bagpipers' music is really cool / loud.
5. Megan's dad and his wife prepared haggis / sausages.

2 A text message

Read Ben's text message to his mum. Then answer the questions.

Lies Bens Nachricht an seine Mutter. Dann beantworte die Fragen.

Mum

This is me with my new cap. 😉
Megan's dad is going to take us to Loch Ness at the weekend. 😊
I hope I'll see the monster!
Tomorrow we'll go to the tourist information centre to get some flyers for B&Bs.

B&B ist die Abkürzung für *bed and breakfast*.
Das ist eine private Unterkunft, in der man übernachten kann und Frühstück bekommt.

Where are they going to go at the weekend?

____

What would Ben like to see?

____

Where will they go tomorrow?

____

3 Giving directions

a) Listen and number the instructions. 42
Höre zu und nummeriere die Anweisungen.

- [ ] turn right at the end
- [ ] turn left at the next corner
- [ ] turn right into
- [1] walk past the church
- [ ] go straight on
- [ ] walk down this road
- [ ] cross the street

b) Read the instructions and match them with the symbols.
Lies die Anweisungen und ordne sie den Symbolen zu.

- [ ] go straight on
- [ ] on your right
- [ ] cross the street
- [ ] turn left
- [ ] walk past
- [ ] turn right
- [ ] on your left

c) Listen to the directions. Follow the way with your finger. 43
Höre dir die Wegbeschreibungen an. Folge dem Weg mit deinem Finger.

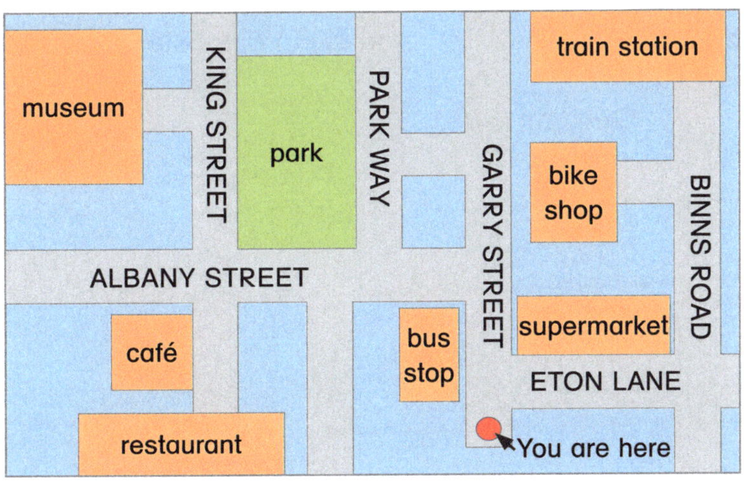

Ihr könnt euch zu zweit auch eigene Wegbeschreibungen ausdenken.

d) Where do you get to? Underline. Wo führt der Weg dich hin? Unterstreiche.

1. to the supermarket / park
2. to the restaurant / train station

5 Where to stay?

a) **Read the flyer. Underline the words you don't know.**
Lies den Flyer. Unterstreiche die Wörter, die du nicht kennst.

Murray House B&B

... for a great stay in the Scottish Highlands

Our B&B in Grotaig offers you a friendly and relaxing atmosphere – and the world's best breakfast.

We have two single rooms, one double room and a family room for three people.

£27 per person per night

The Murray Family and our three dogs are looking forward to your visit.

b) **Look up the words you don't know. Write them in the list.**
Schlage die Wörter nach, die du nicht kennst. Schreibe sie in die Liste.

English word	German word
stay	Aufenthalt

c) **Erzähle einem Partner/einer Partnerin auf Deutsch, was auf dem Flyer steht.**

Es gibt ... Sie haben ...

6 Making a reservation

a) Listen to the phone call. Tick the correct price. 44

Höre dir das Telefonat an. Mache ein Häkchen an den richtigen Preis.

☐ £81 ☐ £110

b) Read the dialogue with a partner. Then make your own dialogue.

Lest den Dialog zu zweit. Dann macht euren eigenen Dialog.

Ann: Hello, this is Ann at Murray House B&B. How can I help you?

Mr McGregor: Hello, this is Ethan McGregor. Have you got two rooms for Friday night?

Ann: Yes, we have.
Would you like single or double rooms?

Mr McGregor: I'd like a single room and a double room.
We're three people.

Ann: That's fine.

Mr McGregor: How much does that cost?

Ann: That's £27 per person so £81 altogether.
Would you like to make a reservation?

Mr McGregor: Yes, please.

Ann: OK, I've made a reservation for this Friday.

Mr McGregor: Perfect. Thank you very much for your help.

Ann: You're welcome. See you on Friday.

Mr McGregor: Bye.

LAND & LEUTE

Loch Ness

Schottland hat viele Seen, die dort *loch* heißen. Loch Ness liegt im schottischen Hochland (*Scottish Highlands*) und ist nach Loch Lomond der zweitgrößte See Schottlands.
Loch Ness ist ein sehr tiefer und dunkler See. Sein Wasser ist auch in der warmen Jahreszeit sehr kalt.
Loch Ness ist weltberühmt, denn in ihm soll angeblich ein Seeungeheuer leben, das *Loch Ness Monster*. Es wird auch liebevoll Nessie genannt.

Hast du schon einmal von Nessie gehört?

7 A trip to Loch Ness

a) **Look at the pictures and listen to the story.** 45
Betrachte die Bilder und höre dir die Geschichte an.

b) **Read the texts and match them with the pictures.**
Lies die Texte und ordne sie den Bildern zu.

1

2

3

4

☐ Later they had a look at the Nessie Shop. And finally there were Loch Ness Monsters everywhere!
"I think I'll get one of these for Fergus," said Megan and picked up a green Nessie toy animal.
"That's a great idea," said Ben.

☐ Then they drove to Urquhart Castle. Ben was very excited.
At the castle, Megan, Ben and Megan's dad climbed to the top of the Grant Tower.

☐ It was Friday morning and Megan, Ben and Megan's dad were on their way from Edinburgh to Loch Ness. Megan and Ben joked about seeing the famous Loch Ness Monster.

☐ After that they had some dinner. Then it was time to say goodbye to Loch Ness and go back to Edinburgh. Maybe they will see the real Nessie next time?!

5

☐ After about four hours they arrived at their B&B in Grotaig. They dropped off their bags.

6

☐ Then they went back to their B&B. "Do you think we'll see Nessie tomorrow?" asked Megan before they went to sleep.
"Don't be silly, Nessie doesn't exist!" answered Ben.

7

☐ Afterwards they went for a walk along the lake. "It's such a lovely day. Why is there no one in the water?" asked Megan.
She put her foot in the water carefully. "Aaaah, that's ice-cold!" she shouted.
"Well, the water is only five degrees all year round," laughed her dad.

8

☐ Early the next morning, Megan, Ben and Megan's dad went on a boat trip. Ben stared at the water excitedly. Suddenly he saw a dark shadow in the water. He screamed and pointed at the shadow.
"It's Nessie!" he shouted.
Megan and her dad looked at the water. "That was only a fish, Ben!" said Megan. The friends looked at each other and started laughing.

c) Work with a partner. Read the first part of the story. Then tell each other what it is about. Go on like this with the other texts.
Arbeitet zu zweit. Lest den ersten Teil der Geschichte. Dann erzählt euch gegenseitig, worum es darin geht. Macht mit den anderen Texten so weiter.

8 The story in short

a) **Put the sentences in the right order.**
Bringe die Sätze in die richtige Reihenfolge.

- [ ] The next morning they went on a boat trip.
- [1] On Friday morning Megan, Ben and Megan's dad went to Loch Ness.
- [ ] Finally they went back to Edinburgh.
- [ ] Afterwards they went for a walk along the lake.
- [ ] First they visited Urquhart Castle.
- [ ] After the boat trip they found lots of little monsters in the Nessie Shop.

b) **Listen and check.** Höre zu und überprüfe. 46

10 Choose an activity

- **Find the words in the monster.** Finde die Wörter im Monster.

- **Make a word monster with words from Theme 5 about Scotland.**
  Erstelle ein Wortmonster mit Wörtern aus Theme 5 über Schottland.

- **Draw a Loch Ness Monster for the Nessie Shop. Then label it.**
  Zeichne ein Loch Ness Monster für den Nessie Shop. Dann beschrifte es.

You can use these words:
Du kannst diese Wörter benutzen:

long | short | big | small | strong | pretty | ugly | friendly | angry | red | green | black | …

head | face | eyes | teeth | legs | tail | …

Present your monster. Stelle dein Monster vor.

11 Target task: Your postcard

a) Match the sentence parts from a postcard.
Ordne die Satzteile von einer Postkarte zu.

Dear	exciting.
Hello from	is great.
It's	Jasmine,
Yesterday we visited	a boat trip.
Today we went on	fantastic here.
We saw the	soon.
It was	Loch Ness Monster, Nessie.
The weather	Loch Ness.
See you	a wonderful castle.

b) Imagine you are Megan or Ben. Write a postcard from Edinburgh. Use a) for help. Stelle dir vor, du bist Megan oder Ben. Schreibe eine Postkarte aus Edinburgh. Nutze a) als Hilfe.

Jasmine Bolt
51 Hartland Road
London
NW1 8DB

c) Read out your postcard to your partner.
Lies deine Postkarte deinem Partner/deiner Partnerin vor.

Theme 1 Are you fit?

Complete the wordbank. Vervollständige die Wortfelder.

Lieblingssportarten: (→ Seite 8-9)

• skateboarding

Wörter und Sätze, um einen Sportler/eine Sportlerin vorzustellen: (→ Seite 10)

• He/She comes from ...

Speisen und Getränke: (→ Seite 14-16)

• vegetables, smoothies

Wörter und Sätze für eine Essensbestellung: (→ Seite 20-21)

• Are you ready to order?

Theme 2 What's on near you?

Complete the wordbank. Vervollständige die Wortfelder.

Dinge, die man auf dem Flohmarkt kaufen kann: (→ Seite 33-34)

• sunglasses

Wörter und Sätze, um ein Verkaufsgespräch zu führen: (→ Seite 34-35)

• Can I help you?

Wörter, die man mit einem Wikingerfestival verbindet: (→ Seite 36-37)

• competition

Wörter, um einen Wikinger/eine Wikingerin zu beschreiben: (→ Seite 40-41)

• helmet

Theme 3 You're not alone

Complete the wordbank. Vervollständige die Wortfelder.

Dinge, die man auf einer einsamen Insel braucht: (→ Seite 45)

- rope

Wörter, um zu sagen, wie man sich fühlt: (→ Seite 48)

- excited

Wörter und Sätze, die mit Streit und Problemen zu tun haben: (→ Seite 52-56)

- argue

Was man machen kann, wenn man Probleme hat: (→ Seite 59)

- You can talk to a friend.

Theme 4 Everyday science

Complete the wordbank. Vervollständige die Wortfelder.

Was man mit dem Computer oder Handy machen kann: (→ Seite 62, 67)

- send emails

Erfindungen: (→ Seite 68-70)

- bike

Dinge, die Strom brauchen: (→ Seite 74)

- toaster

Dinge, die man ohne Strom nicht machen kann: (→ Seite 74)

- watch TV

Theme 5 Up and away

Complete the wordbank. Vervollständige die Wortfelder.

Was es an einem Bahnhof gibt: (→ Seite 86)

- ticket office

Sätze, die du am Fahrkartenschalter sagen kannst: (→ Seite 88-89)

- Two return tickets to Bristol, please.

Wörter und Sätze, um den Weg zu beschreiben: (→ Seite 91)

- turn left

Sätze, die du bei einer Hotelreservierung sagen kannst: (→ Seite 93)

- I'd like a single room.

Auf den folgenden Seiten kannst du noch einmal nachschlagen, wie du etwas auf Englisch sagen kannst.

1 So kannst du über dich selbst Auskunft geben:

My name is Jasmine.

I am twelve years old. / **I'm** twelve years old.

I am from Leeds. / **I'm** from Leeds.

2 So kannst du über eine andere Person Auskunft geben:

His name is Sandeep.

He is from England.

His hobby is football.

He **has got** brown eyes.

He **hates** baked beans.

Her name is Megan.

She is twelve years old.

Her hobby is dancing.

She **likes** orange juice.

She **plays** rugby.

3 So sagst du, ob du etwas hast oder besitzt:

I **have got** a dog. / I**'ve got** a dog.

I **haven't got** a pencil.

4 So fragst du, ob jemand etwas hat:

Have you **got** a ruler?

5 So kannst du beschreiben, was es (irgendwo) gibt:

There is a chair.

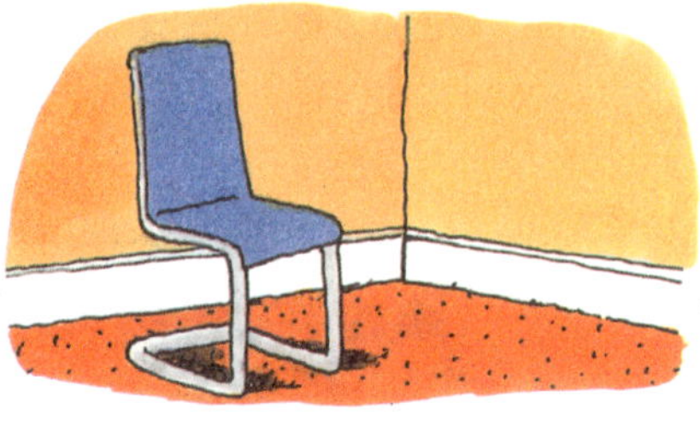

There are two chairs.

6 So sagst du, wem (oder zu wem) etwas gehört:

Megan**'s** birthday is in May.

Ben**'s** budgies are green and yellow.

Jasmine**'s** brother is called Jason.

7 So sagst du, ob du etwas magst:

☺ I **like** jam.

☹ I **don't like** cheese.

8 So fragst du, ob jemand etwas mag:

Do you **like** tennis? – Yes, I do. / No, I don't.

9 So sprichst du von mehreren Dingen oder Personen:

1 girl  → 2 girl**s** 

1 football  → 2 football**s** 

10 So sagst du, wo genau sich etwas befindet:

The smiley is **on** the box. 

The smiley is **under** the box. 

The smiley is **next to** the box. 

The smiley is **in front of** the box. 

11 So sagst du, wie häufig du etwas tust.

I **always** take out the rubbish.

I **often** lay the table.

I **sometimes** tidy my room.

I **never** make my bed.

12 So sagst du, ob du etwas tun kannst:

I **can play** the guitar.

I **can't play** tennis.

13 So sagst du, was du gerade (in diesem Moment) tust:

I **am playing** football. / I'**m playing** football.

14 So sagst du, was andere gerade tun:

Jason **is listening** to music.

The boys **are playing** football.

15 So kannst du sagen, was schon passiert ist (zum Beispiel gestern, letzte Woche oder letztes Jahr):

My grandma **played** video games **yesterday**.

Jasmine **was** in Leeds **last week**.

I **went** to France **last year**.

Wenn etwas nicht passiert ist, sagst du:

I **didn't** play basketball.

He **didn't** go to the cinema.

Fragen stellst du so:

Did you **go** to the beach yesterday? – Yes, I did. / No, I didn't.

What **did** you **do** yesterday? – I went to a party.

16 So vergleichst du Sachen, Tiere und Personen miteinander:

The dog is **small**.

The cat is **smaller**.

The mouse is **the smallest**.

An elephant is **bigger than** a dog.

17 So kannst du sagen, was in der Zukunft passieren wird:

I **will** have a good job in twenty years.

So kürzt du *will* ab:

I**'ll** have a wife and two children.

Wenn etwas nicht passieren wird, sagst du:

I **won't** live in London.

She **won't** be famous.

18 So kannst du ausdrücken, wie man etwas macht:

He sings **loudly**.

The cow is running **fast**.

The dog barks **angrily**.

19 So sagst du, dass jemand etwas tun muss oder nicht tun darf:

Ben **must** tidy his room.

I **must** go to school.

You **mustn't** eat too much chocolate.

I **mustn't** steal Jasmine's lunchbox.

20 So sagst du, ob jemand schon etwas getan hat:

I **have already decorated** the room.

They **have already done** the shopping.

He **hasn't done** his homework **yet**.

21 So kannst du sagen, was jemand für die Zukunft plant:

I'm **going to** watch a film tomorrow.

Megan **is going to** go to a party at the weekend.

A

a/an	ein(e)	**a** dog / **an** animal
a lot (of)	viel(e); sehr	
about	über; ungefähr; an	
accessible	(leicht) erreichbar; behindertengerecht	
act out	nachspielen	
activity	Aktivität	1 **activity** – 2 activities
address	Adresse	
advice	Rat(schlag)	
African	Afrikaner/in; afrikanisch	
after	nach	**after** school – nach der Schule
after that	anschließend, danach	
afternoon	Nachmittag	
in the afternoon	am Nachmittag, nachmittags	
afterwards	danach, anschließend; später	
again	wieder, noch (ein)mal	Read the text **again**. – Lies den Text noch einmal.
against	gegen	
age	Alter	
aggressive	aggressiv; energisch	
(three years) ago	vor (drei Jahren)	
agony aunt	Briefkastentante; Kummerkastentante	
agree on	einer Meinung sein über; sich einigen auf	
air	Luft	
all	alle(s)	
all my life	mein ganzes Leben	
all over	überall in/auf	
all over the world	auf der ganzen Welt	
all year	das ganze Jahr (über)	
all year round	das ganze Jahr über	
alone	allein	
along	entlang	
already	schon	I have **already** eaten. – Ich habe schon gegessen.
also	auch	
altogether	völlig, ganz; insgesamt	
always	immer	
am	bin	
a.m.	morgens, vormittags	9 **a.m.** – 9 Uhr morgens
amazing	toll, unglaublich	
and	und	
angry	verärgert; zornig; wütend	
animal	Tier	
announcement	Durchsage; Ansage	
another	noch ein(e, r, s); ein(e) andere(r, s)	I would like another drink. – Ich möchte noch ein Getränk.

answer	(be)antworten; Antwort	
any	irgendwelche, irgendein(e)	
not anymore	nicht mehr	
anyone	jede/r; (irgend)jemand	Is **anyone** there? – Ist jemand da?
anything	(irgend)(et)was	
anything else	(irgend)(et)was anderes	
anywhere	überall (hin); irgendwo (hin)	
apple	Apfel	
apple crumble	Apfelauflauf	
apple juice	Apfelsaft	I **am** – ich bin
are	bist, sind, seid	you **are** – du bist
area	Gebiet, Region	he / she / it **is** – er / sie / es ist
aren't (= are not)	du bist nicht; ihr seid nicht; wir/sie sind nicht	we **are** – wir sind you **are** – ihr seid
argue	sich streiten	they **are** – sie sind
around	um	
arrival	Ankunft	
arrive	ankommen	They **arrive** at 9 a.m. – Sie kommen um 9 Uhr an.
article	Artikel	
as	als; wie	
as ... as	(genau)so ... wie ...	
as usual	wie üblich, wie gewöhnlich	
ask	fragen; bitten	
ask for	bitten um	He **asked** me **for** help. – Er hat mich um Hilfe gebeten.
at	auf, an, in, bei; um	
at all	überhaupt	
at least	mindestens, wenigstens	
the Atlantic (Ocean)	Atlantischer Ozean	
atmosphere	Atmosphäre; Stimmung	
available	verfügbar; erhältlich	
away	weg	
axe	Axt; Beil	

B

B&B (= bed and breakfast)	Frühstückspension	
back	Rücken; Rückseite; zurück	
backwards	rückwärts	
bad	schlecht	
bag	Tasche	Where is my **bag**? – Wo ist meine Tasche?
bagpiper	Dudelsackspieler/in	
balance	das Gleichgewicht halten	
balance on one leg	auf einem Bein balancieren	
balloon	Ballon	
banana	Banane	
basket	Korb	
battle	Kampf; Schlacht	
be	sein	
be about	handeln von	The text **is about** Vikings. – Der Text handelt von Wikingern.

beach	Strand	I like going to the **beach**. – Ich mag es, zum Strand zu gehen.
beard	Bart	
beautiful	schön	
because	weil	
bed	Bett	
been	siehe „be“	I have **been** to London. – Ich bin schon mal in London gewesen.
before	vor	
began	Vergangenheitsform von „begin“	
begin	anfangen, beginnen	
below	unten; unter(halb)	Look at the pictures **below**. – Sieh dir die Bilder unten an.
best	beste(r, s); am meisten/ liebsten/besten	
best wishes	viele Grüße	
better	besser; lieber, mehr	
big	groß	
bike	(Fahr)rad	
bill	Rechnung	
biology	Biologie	**Biology** is my favourite subject. – Biologie ist mein Lieblingsfach.
bird	Vogel	
a bit	ein bisschen	
black	schwarz	
blood-red	blutrot	
blue	blau	
boat	Boot; Schiff	
boat trip	Bootsfahrt	
book	Buch	
booklet	Broschüre	
bored	gelangweilt	
boring	langweilig	
born	geboren	
borrow	leihen	Can I **borrow** your pen? – Kann ich deinen Stift leihen?
bottle	Flasche	
at the bottom (of)	unten, am unteren Ende (von)	
bought	Vergangenheitsform von „buy“	
boy	Junge	
boyfriend	(fester) Freund	
bread	Brot	
breakfast	Frühstück	
bring	(mit)bringen	
British	britische(r, s)	
brother	Bruder	I have an older **brother**. – Ich habe einen älteren Bruder.
brought	Vergangenheitsform von „bring“	
brush	bürsten; putzen	
budgie	Wellensittich	
build	bauen	

bus driver	Busfahrer/in	
bus stop	Bushaltestelle	Where is the nearest **bus stop**? Wo ist die nächste Bushaltestelle?
but	aber	
buy	kaufen	
buyer	Käufer/in	
by	bei, in der Nähe; nach; mit, durch; von	
by (bus)	mit (dem Bus)	I go to school **by bus**. – Ich fahre mit dem Bus zur Schule.
bye	tschüss	

C

cake	Kuchen	
cake sale	Kuchenverkauf	
call	(an)rufen; nennen	
came	Vergangenheitsform von „come“	
can	können	I **can** hear a dog. – Ich kann einen Hund hören.
can't (= cannot)	nicht können	
can	Dose	
cap	Mütze, Kappe	
cape	Umhang	
capital (city)	Hauptstadt	
captain	Kapitän/in	
car	Auto	
car boot sale	Verkauf persönlicher Gegenstände aus dem Kofferraum auf einem Parkplatz	
careful	vorsichtig; sorgfältig	Please be **careful**! – Seid bitte vorsichtig!
carefully	vorsichtig	
the Carribean	die Karibik	
carrier	Träger; Transporter	
carve	schnitzen	
cash machine	Geldautomat	
castle	Burg, Schloss	
cat	Katze	
catch	fangen	
cave	Höhle	
century	Jahrhundert	We are in the 21st **century**. – Wir sind im 21. Jahrhundert.
cereal	Getreide(sorte); Frühstückszerealien	
certainly	sicher(lich), bestimmt, gewiss	
change	(sich) verändern; Veränderung; Wechselgeld	
chant	singen, im Sprechchor rufen	
charity	Wohltätigkeitsorganisation; wohltätige Zwecke	

charity run	Spendenlauf, Sponsorenlauf	
chat	plaudern; chatten	
cheap	billig, preiswert	
check	überprüfen, kontrollieren	
cheer up	aufmuntern; aufheitern	
chicken	Huhn; Hähnchen	
child/children	Kind/Kinder	1 **child** – 2 **children**
chips	Pommes frites	
chocolate cake	Schokoladenkuchen	
chocolate chip cookie	Keks mit Schokoladenstückchen	
chocolate	Schokolade	
choice	Wahl	
choose	auswählen	Please **choose** a number. – Wähle bitte eine Zahl aus.
chosen	siehe „choose“	
Christmas market	Weihnachtsmarkt	
Christmas play	Weihnachtsspiel	
church	Kirche	
cinema	Kino	I went to the **cinema** yesterday. – Ich ging gestern ins Kino.
circle	einkreisen, umkringeln	
city	(Groß)stadt	
class	(Schul)klasse	
class trip	Klassenfahrt	
classmate	Klassenkamerad/in, Mitschüler/in	
classroom	Klassenzimmer	Our **classroom** is quite big. – Unser Klassenzimmer ist ziemlich groß.
clean	sauber machen, reinigen, putzen	
clever	klug, gescheit, schlau	
climb	klettern	
close	schließen, zumachen	
close down	schließen, stilllegen	
clothes	Kleider, Kleidung	
coffee	Kaffee	
collect	sammeln	
colour	färben, anmalen; Farbe	My favourite **colour** is yellow. – Meine Lieblingsfarbe ist Gelb.
colourful	farbenfroh, farbenprächtig	
come	kommen	
comment	Kommentar, Bemerkung	
communication	Kommunikation	
compare	vergleichen	
competition	Wettbewerb	
complete	vervollständigen, ergänzen	**Complete** the sentences. – Vervollständige die Sätze.
concert	Konzert	
connect	verbinden	
cook	kochen	
copy	abschreiben	
corner	Ecke	

correct	richtig, korrekt	Circle the **correct** answer. – Kreise die richtige Antwort ein.
cost	kosten	
costume	Tracht, Kostüm	
cotton	Baumwolle	
could	könnte(st, n, t)	
couldn't (= could not)	konnte(st, n, t) nicht; könnte(st, n, t) nicht	I **couldn't** see you. – Ich konnte dich nicht sehen.
country	Land	
cow	Kuh	
create	erschaffen; gestalten	
crisps	Chips	
cross	überqueren; durchqueren	
Crown Jewels	Kronjuwelen	
culture	Kultur	
cup	Tasse	
curry	Curry(gericht)	
cute	süß, niedlich	
cycling	Radfahren, Radeln	

D

dad	Papa, Vati	My **dad** is very funny. – Mein Papa ist sehr lustig.
daffodil	Osterglocke; gelbe Narzisse	
dangerous	gefährlich	
dark	dunkel	
date	Datum	What's the **date** today? – Was ist heute für ein Datum?
daughter	Tochter	
day	Tag	
deal with	sich befassen mit; umgehen mit	
dear	liebe(r) (*Anrede*)	
December	Dezember	
decorate	schmücken, dekorieren	We have **decorated** the tree. – Wir haben den Baum geschmückt.
degree	Grad	
delete	streichen, löschen	
delicious	köstlich, lecker	
Denmark	Dänemark	
departure	Abreise; Abflug; Abfahrt	
desert island	einsame Insel	
design	entwerfen	
dessert	Nachtisch, Dessert	Would you like a **dessert**? – Möchtest du einen Nachtisch?
dialogue	Dialog, Gespräch	
diary	Tagebuch	
did	Vergangenheitsform von „do“	
didn't (= did not)	Vergangenheitsform von „do not“	
difference	Unterschied	
different	anders, verschieden	

dinner	Abendessen; Mittagessen	What did you have for **dinner**? – Was hast du zu Abend gegessen?
direct	direkt	
direction	Richtung	
discovery	Entdeckung	
disgusting	widerlich	
dish/dishes	Gericht/Gerichte	
dishwasher	Geschirrspülmaschine	
dispenser	Automat; Spender	
display	Display, Bildschirm	
distance	Entfernung; Strecke	
do	machen, tun	
does	er/sie/es macht	
doesn't (= does not)	er/sie/es macht nicht	
dog	Hund	
don't (= do not)	ich mache nicht; du machst nicht; wir/sie machen nicht; ihr macht nicht	
done	siehe „do“	I have **done** my homework. – Ich habe meine Hausaufgaben gemacht.
done	gemacht; fertig, erledigt	
door	Tür	
double	doppelt, Doppel-	
double room	Doppelzimmer	
down	(nach) unten; hinunter, hinab	
download	herunterladen, downloaden	
dragon	Drache	
draw	zeichnen; ziehen	
dream	Traum	
dress up (as)	sich verkleiden (als)	He **dressed up as** a Viking. – Er hat sich als Wikinger verkleidet.
drink	trinken	
drink	Getränk	
drive	fahren	
drop off	abliefern, absetzen	
drove	Vergangenheitsform von „drive“	
drunk	siehe „drink“	She has **drunk** her tea. – Sie hat ihren Tee getrunken.
during	während	

E

each	jede(r, s)	
each other	einander	
early	früh	
earn	verdienen	
earring	Ohrring	I like your **earrings**! – Ich mag deine Ohrringe!
Easter fire	Osterfeuer	
easy	einfach; leicht	
eat	essen	
eaten	siehe „eat“	

eating habits	Essgewohnheiten	
eating out	Essen gehen	
egg	Ei	
Egypt	Ägypten	
eight	acht	
eighteen	achtzehn	
electricity	Elektrizität; Strom	A computer needs **electricity**. – Ein Rechner braucht Strom.
electronic (music)	Elektro; Elektromusik	
elephant	Elefant	
else	sonst, anders	
embarassing	peinlich	
empty	ausräumen, (ent)leeren	
end	enden; Ende	
end in a draw	unentschieden ausgehen/ enden	The game **ended in a draw**. – Das Spiel ging unentschieden aus.
ending	Ende, Schluss	
English	Englisch; englisch	
enjoy	mögen; genießen	
Enjoy your meal!	Guten Appetit!	
enough	genügend, ausreichend, genug	
entry	Eintritt; Zugang; Eintrag	
escalator	Rolltreppe	
Europe	Europa	Germany is in **Europe**. – Deutschland liegt in Europa.
European	Europäer/in; europäisch	
even	selbst; sogar	
evening	Abend	
ever	jemals	
every	jede(r, s)	I play football **every** Friday. – Ich spiele jeden Freitag Fußball.
everyday	alltäglich, Alltags-; im Alltag	
everyone	jede(r); alle	
everything	alles	
everywhere	überall	
excited	aufgeregt	
excitedly	aufgeregt	
exciting	aufregend; spannend	
exercise	Übung, Aufgabe	Please do **exercise** 3. – Mach bitte Aufgabe 3.
exist	existieren, vorkommen	
experience	Erfahrung	
eye	Auge	

F

face	Gesicht	
face paint	Gesichtsfarbe	
fact	Fakt	
fact file	Steckbrief	
fall	fallen	
false	falsch	

family	Familie	
family member	Familienmitglied	
famous	berühmt	
fantastic	fantastisch, wunderbar	The concert was **fantastic**! – Das Konzert war fantastisch!
far	weit	
farm	Bauernhof	
fashion	Mode	
fast	schnell	
father	Vater	
favourite	Lieblings-	
fear	(be)fürchten	
February	Februar	My birthday is in **February**. – Mein Geburtstag ist im Februar.
fed	Vergangenheitsform von „feed“	
feed	füttern, zu Essen geben	
feel	(sich) fühlen	
fell	Vergangenheitsform von „fall“	
felt	Vergangenheitsform von „feel“	
festival	Fest; Festival	
fifteen	fünfzehn	**fifteen** – 15
fifty	fünfzig	**fifty** – 50
fight	kämpfen, streiten	
fill in	ausfüllen, eintragen	**Fill in** the gaps. – Fülle die Lücken aus.
film	filmen, drehen	
finally	schließlich, endlich; zum Schluss	
find	finden	
find out	herausfinden	
finder	Finder/in	
fine	in Ordnung, gut	
fire	Feuer; (ab)feuern, schießen	
fireworks	Feuerwerk	
first	erste(r, s); zuerst, als Erstes	
fish	fischen, angeln	
fish	Fisch/Fische	1 **fish** – 2 **fish**
fishing	Angeln, Fischen	
five	fünf	
flag	Fahne; Flagge	
flea market	Flohmarkt; Trödelmarkt	
floor	Boden	
flower	Blume	
follow	folgen	**Follow** me! – Folge mir!
follower	Anhänger/in; Follower/in	
food	Essen; Futter	
foot/feet	Fuß/Füße	

football	Fußball	
football match	Fußballspiel	
for	für; zum; nach	
for example	zum Beispiel	
forget	vergessen	
forgotten	siehe „forget“	I have **forgotten** my homework. – Ich habe meine Hausaufgaben vergessen.
forty	vierzig	
found	Vergangenheitsform von „find“	
four	vier	
fourteen	vierzehn	
free	frei	
Friday	Freitag	
fridge	Kühlschrank	
friend	Freund/in	
friendly	freundlich	
friendly match	Freundschaftsspiel	
from	von, aus	They are **from** Frankfurt. – Sie sind aus Frankfurt.
front	Vorderseite	
fruit	Frucht; Obst	
fruit juice	(Frucht)saft	
frustrated	frustriert; enttäuscht	
fun	Spaß; lustig, witzig, spaßig	
be fun	Spaß machen	The party **was fun**! – Die Party hat Spaß gemacht!
funny	lustig, witzig, komisch	
further	zusätzlich, noch mehr, weiter	
future	Zukunft	

G

Gaelic	Gälisch; gälisch	
gallery	Galerie; Ausstellung	
game	Spiel	
garlic	Knoblauch	
gave	Vergangenheitsform von „give“	He **gave** me a present. – Er gab mir ein Geschenk.
German	Deutsch; deutsch	
Germany	Deutschland	
get	erhalten, bekommen; (an)kommen; steigen	**Get** well soon! – Gute Besserung!
get to know	kennenlernen	
get ready	sich bereit machen	
get (to)	(an)kommen	
girl	Mädchen	
give	geben	
give a helping hand	helfen; behilflich sein	
give directions	den Weg beschreiben	She **gave** me **directions**. – Sie hat mir den Weg beschrieben.
glad	glücklich, froh	
glass	Glas	

glass front	Vorderseite aus Glas	
go	gehen	
go cycling	radfahren gehen	
go for a walk	spazieren gehen	I am **going for a walk**. – Ich gehe spazieren.
go hiking	wandern gehen	
go on	weitergehen; weitermachen	
go skating	skaten gehen	
go to sleep	schlafen gehen, einschlafen	
go swimming	schwimmen gehen	
goal	Tor	
goalkeeper	Tormann; Torfrau	
goes	er/sie/es geht	
going to	werden	I am **going to call my friend**. – Ich werde meinen Freund anrufen.
gone	siehe „go“	
good	gut	
good-looking	gut aussehend	
goodbye	auf Wiedersehen	
got	Vergangenheitsform von „get“	
grand	groß, großartig	
grandfather	Großvater	My **grandma** and **grandfather** are my **grandparents**. – Meine Oma und mein Opa sind meine Großeltern.
grandma	Oma; Omi	
grandparents	Großeltern	
great	großartig, toll	
green	grün	
grey	grau	
group	Gruppe	
guinea pig	Meerschweinchen	
guitar	Gitarre	She can play the **guitar** well. – Sie kann gut Gitarre spielen.
gun	(Schuss)waffe, Kanone	
guys	Leute	
gymnastics	Turnen	

H

habit	Gewohnheit	
had	Vergangenheitsform von „have“	I **had** a great day. – Ich hatte einen tollen Tag.
haggis	schottisches Gericht aus gekochten Schafsinnereien	
hairdryer	Föhn	
half brother	Halbbruder	Adam is my **half brother**. – Adam ist mein Halbbruder.
hall	Halle; Saal	
handball match	Handballspiel	
happen	geschehen, passieren	
happy	glücklich; zufrieden; fröhlich	
hard	hart; schwer	
harp	Harfe	

has	hat	
has got	hat	He **has got** brown eyes. – Er hat braune Augen.
hate	hassen, nicht ausstehen können	
have	haben; essen	
have a look (at)	(sich) (an)schauen	
Have a nice day!	Viel Spaß!; Einen schönen Tag noch!	
have a party	eine Party feiern	
have breakfast	frühstücken	
have got	haben	
have to	müssen	I **have to** tidy my room. – Ich muss mein Zimmer aufräumen.
haven't (= have not)	nicht haben	
he	er	
head	Kopf	
heading	Überschrift; Titel	
health	Gesundheit	
healthy	gesund	
hear	hören	
heard	Vergangenheitsform von „hear"	Have you **heard** the news? – Hast du die Neuigkeiten gehört?
heart	Herz	
hello	hallo	
helmet	Helm	
help	Hilfe; helfen	
help out	(aus)helfen, unterstützen	
helping	hilfreich; helfend	
helpless	hilflos	
helpline	telefonischer Beratungsdienst; Notruf	
her	ihr(e, n); sie	That is **her** pen, not yours. – Das ist ihr Stift, nicht deiner.
here	hier(her)	
Here you are.	Hier, bitte!, Bitte schön!	
here's (= here is)	hier ist	
hi	hallo, hi	
high	hoch	
highest	höchste(r, s)	
the (Scottish) Highlands	(schottisches) Hochland; Highlands	
hiking	Wandern	
him	ihm, ihn	
himself	sich (selbst); selbst	He did it **himself**. – Er hat es selbst gemacht.
his	sein(e, r)	
history	Geschichte	
hit	schlagen; treffen; stoßen (gegen); erschüttern	
hockey stick	Hockeyschläger	
hold	(fest)halten	
holiday	Urlaub, Ferien	

home	zu Hause; nach Hause	
feel homesick	Heimweh haben	
homework	Hausaufgaben	
honest	ehrlich	Please be **honest**. – Sei bitte ehrlich.
honey	Honig	
hope	hoffen	
horse	Pferd	
hot	heiß	It is usually **hot** in August. – Es ist normalerweise heiß im August.
hour	Stunde	
house	Haus	
how	wie	
How are you?	Wie geht es dir/Ihnen/ euch?	
How much is/are ... ?	Was kostet/kosten ...?	
how to	wie man	
hundred	hundert	
hurry	sich beeilen, hetzen	I'm late! I have to **hurry**. – Ich bin spät dran! Ich muss mich beeilen.
husband	Ehemann	
hut	Hütte	

I

I	ich	
I don't think so.	Das glaube ich nicht.	
I'd (= I would)	ich würde	
I'd like ...	ich hätte gern ...	**I'd like** a lemonade, please. – Ich hätte gerne eine Limonade.
I'd like (to)	ich würde gern ...	
I'll (= I will)	ich werde	
I'm (= I am)	ich bin, ich heiße	
I'm sorry	Das tut mir leid.	
I've got (= I have got)	ich habe	
ice cream	Eiscreme	
ice-cold	eiskalt	
idea	Idee	
if	wenn, falls	
ignore	ignorieren	
imagine	sich vorstellen	
important	wichtig	My family is very **important**. – Meine Familie ist sehr wichtig.
in person	persönlich	
in short	kurz gesagt	
in surprise	erstaunt; überrascht	
include	beinhalten, einschließen	
India	Indien	
industrial	industriell, Industrie-	
industry	Industrie	
information point	Informationsstelle	
innovation	Innovation; (Er)neuerung	
inside	drinnen; innen	Let's eat **inside**. – Lass uns drinnen essen.
instead (of)	stattdessen; (an)statt	
instruction	Anweisung, Anleitung	

interesting	interessant
into	in
invent	erfinden
invention	Erfindung
inventor	Erfinder/in
Ireland	Irland
Irish	Irisch; irisch
is	ist
island	Insel
isn't (= is not)	ist nicht
it	es
it's (= it is)	es ist
Italian	Italienisch; italienisch
item	Gegenstand, Artikel, Ding

The smartphone is a great **invention**. – Das Smartphone ist eine tolle Erfindung.

J

jack-o'-lantern	Kürbislaterne
jacket	Jacke
joke	Witz; scherzen
juice	Saft
jump	springen
June	Juni
just	gleich; nur; einfach; gerade

I know a good **joke**. – Ich kenne einen guten Witz.

K

keep	(be)halten
kettle	Wasserkocher
kid	Kind
kilt	Kilt, Schottenrock
kind	Art, Sorte
knife/knives	Messer
know	wissen; kennen

Do you **know** my sister? – Kennst du meine Schwester?

L

label	beschriften
lake	See
lane	Gasse, enge Straße
language	Sprache
large	groß
largest	größte(r, s)
last	letzte(r, s)
late	(zu) spät
later	später
laugh	lachen
learn	lernen
learn by heart	auswendig lernen
leave	verlassen; da lassen; abfahren

The train **leaves** at 2 p.m. – Der Zug fährt um 14 Uhr ab.

left	Vergangenheitsform von „leave“	
left	übrig; (nach) links	
on the/your left	links, auf der/deiner linken Seite	The church is **on the left**. – Die Kirche ist auf der linken Seite.
leg	Bein	
lemonade	Limonade	
let	lassen	
let's (= let us)	lass(t) uns	
Let's go!	Los!, Auf geht's!	
letter	Brief; Buchstabe	
library	Bibliothek, Bücherei	
life/lives	Leben	1 **life** – 2 **lives**
lift	(hoch)heben; Aufzug; Lift	
light	erhellen, erleuchten	
light bulb	Glühbirne	
like	mögen; wie	
line	Linie; Zeile	
lion	Löwe	
list	Liste	
listen (to)	(zu)hören	My mum is **listening to** music. – Meine Mama hört Musik.
little	klein	
live	leben, wohnen	
living room	Wohnzimmer	
loch	See	
lonely	einsam	
long	lang	
look	sehen, schauen; aussehen	
look at	betrachten, sehen, anschauen	**Look at** that beautiful picture! – Schau dir das schöne Bild an!
look for	suchen (nach)	
look forward to	sich freuen auf	
look up	nachschlagen	
lose	verlieren	
lost	Vergangenheitsform von „lose“	I have **lost** my ruler. – Ich habe mein Lineal verloren.
a lot (of)	sehr; viel(e)	
lots of	viel, jede Menge	
loud	laut	
love	lieben; sehr gern mögen	
lovely	schön, hübsch	
lunch	Mittagessen	
lyrics	(Lied)text	I don't know the **lyrics**. – Ich kenne den Liedtext nicht.

M

machine	Maschine	
madam	gnädige Frau (*Anrede*)	
made	Vergangenheitsform von „make“	

made	gemacht, hergestellt	
made of	(gemacht) aus	My desk is **made of** wood. – Mein Schreibtisch ist aus Holz.
main	Haupt-	
main course	Hauptgericht; Hauptgang	
make	machen; erstellen	
make notes	(sich) Notizen machen	
make up	(sich) ausdenken, erfinden	
making	Herstellung	
man/men	Mann/Männer	1 **man** – 2 **men**
many	viele	
map	(Land)karte	
March	März	
mark	(Schul)note	
marry	heiraten	
match	Spiel; Streichholz, Zündholz	
match (with)	zuordnen	**Match** the sentences. – Ordne die Sätze zu.
matching	(zusammen)passend	
maybe	vielleicht	
maze	Labyrinth, Irrgarten	
me	mir, mich	
meal	Mahlzeit; Essen	
mean	gemein, fies	
meat	Fleisch	I don't eat **meat**. – Ich esse kein Fleisch.
meet	(sich) treffen; kennenlernen	
melody	Melodie	
member	Mitglied	
menu	Speisekarte	
message	Nachricht	
met	Vergangenheitsform von „meet"	I **met** my friends in the park yesterday. – Ich habe gestern meine Freunde im Park getroffen.
metal	Metall	
metre	Meter	
microwave	Mikrowelle	
in the middle	in der Mitte; mitten in/auf	
might	könnte	
milk	Milch	
mirror	Spiegel	
miss	verpassen; vermissen	
mobile (phone)	Mobiltelefon, Handy	
Monday	Montag	
money	Geld	
monoplane	Eindecker	
month	Monat	
more	(noch) mehr	
morning	Morgen	Good **morning**! – Guten Morgen!
most	die meisten; am meisten	
mother	Mutter	
mountain	Berg	

move	sich bewegen; umziehen	
Mr	Herr (*Anrede*)	Dear **Mr** Robinson ... – Lieber Herr Robinson ...
Mrs	Frau (*Anrede*)	Dear **Mrs** McDonald ... – Liebe Frau McDonald ...
much	viel; sehr	
mum	Mama, Mutti	
music	Musik	
my	mein(e)	
myself	mich, mir; selbst	

N

national team	Nationalmannschaft	
near	nah(e); in der Nähe	
need	brauchen	I **need** a red pen. – Ich brauche einen roten Stift.
nervous	nervös; aufgeregt	
net	Netz	
never	nie(mals)	
new	neu	
next	nächste(r, s)	**next** week – nächste Woche **next** month – nächsten Monat **next** year – nächstes Jahr
the next morning	am nächsten Morgen	
next to	neben	
nice	nett; schön	
night	Nacht	
nine	neun	
nineteen	neunzehn	
no	nein; kein(e)	
no more	nie wieder	
no one	keine(r), niemand	
normally	normalerweise	I **normally** get home at 3 p.m. – Ich komme normalerweise um 15 Uhr nach Hause.
Northern Ireland	Nordirland	
nose	Nase	
not	nicht	
note	Notiz; Note; Ton; Klang	
now	jetzt	
number	nummerieren; Zahl, Ziffer, Nummer	

O

(eight) o'clock	(acht) Uhr	
October	Oktober	Halloween is on 31st **October**. – Halloween ist am 31. Oktober.
odd one out	fünftes Rad am Wagen	
of	von	
of course	natürlich	
offer	Angebot; (an)bieten	
office	Büro	
official	offiziell, amtlich	
often	oft, häufig	
old	alt	
on	auf, an; in; am; für	
once	einmal	

one	eins; ein(e)	
only	nur	
open	offen, geöffnet; (sich) öffnen, aufmachen	The shop **opens** at 8 a.m. – Der Laden öffnet um 8 Uhr.
open up	(sich) öffnen	
open-air	im Freien, Open-Air	
opening hours	Öffnungszeiten	
or	oder	
orange	Orange, Apfelsine; orange(farben)	
orange juice	Orangensaft	I drink **orange juice** every morning. – Ich trinke jeden Morgen Orangensaft.
order	bestellen; Ordnung, Reihenfolge	
organise	organisieren	
other	andere(r, s)	
our	unser(e)	
out	nach draußen, (he)raus	
outside	im Freien, draußen	
over	hinüber, herüber	
over there	dort (drüben)	The toilets are **over there**. – Die Toiletten sind dort drüben.
own	eigene(r, s)	

P

page	Seite	
paint	(an)malen	
pair	Paar	Please work in **pairs**. – Arbeitet bitte zu zweit.
palm tree	Palme	
paper	Papier	
parents	Eltern	
part	Teil	
password	Passwort	
past	vorbei/vorüber an	
pasta	Nudeln	
pea	Erbse	
pencil	Bleistift	
people	Leute, Menschen	
per	pro	
perfect	perfekt	
personal	persönlich; privat	
pet	Haustier	
phone	Telefon; anrufen	
phone call	(Telefon)anruf	
phone case	Handyhülle	I have bought a **phone case** for my mobile phone. – Ich habe eine Handyhülle für mein Handy gekauft.
photo	Foto	
pick up	aufheben; erwerben	
picture	Bild, Foto	
piece of paper	Blatt Papier, Zettel	
pioneer	Pionier/in; Wegbereiter/in	
place	Ort; Platz	

plan	planen	
plane	Flugzeug	I took a **plane** to Spain. – Ich bin mit dem Flugzeug nach Spanien geflogen.
plastic	Plastik; Kunststoff	
plate	Teller	
platform	Bahnsteig; Plattform	
play	spielen	
player	Spieler/in	
playground	Spielplatz	
playing	Spielen	
please	bitte	
p.m.	nachmittags, abends	8 **p.m.** – 8 Uhr abends / 20 Uhr
pocket money	Taschengeld	
poem	Gedicht	
point (at)	zeigen/deuten (auf)	
possible	möglich	as soon as **possible** – so bald wie möglich
post	schicken; ins Internet stellen, posten	
post	Post; Beitrag auf einer Social-Media-Plattform, in einem Blog oder Forum	
postcard	Postkarte	
potato/potatoes	Kartoffel/Kartoffeln	
pound	Pfund *(brit. Währung)*	A coffee costs 2 **pounds**. – Ein Kaffee kostet 2 Pfund.
practise	üben	
prefer	vorziehen, bevorzugen, lieber mögen	
prepare	(sich) vorbereiten	
present	präsentieren	
press	drücken	
pretty	hübsch	
price	Preis	
prize	Preis; Gewinn	
programme	Programm; Sendung	
pumpkin	Kürbis	
punch	Punsch; Bowle	
put	setzen, legen, stellen	Can you please **put** the plates on the table? – Kannst du bitte die Teller auf den Tisch stellen?
put in order	in Ordnung bringen, ordnen	
put on	anziehen; auftragen	
put up	aufhängen	

Q

question	Frage
quickly	schnell

R

rainwater	Regenwasser
raise	beschaffen, aufbringen/ auftreiben

raise money	Geld aufbringen/auftreiben	
reaction	Reaktion	
read	lesen	
read along	mitlesen	
read out	(laut) vorlesen	
reading	Lesen; Lesung	
ready	fertig, bereit	Are you **ready**? – Bist du bereit?
real	wirklich; echt	
really	wirklich	
recipe	Rezept	
red	rot	
relax	sich entspannen	
relaxing	entspannend	
repeat	wiederholen	Can you please **repeat** that? – Kannst du das bitte wiederholen?
rescue	retten	
reservation	Reservierung	
return (ticket)	Rückfahrkarte	
rhythm	Rhythmus; Takt	
rice	Reis	
ride	fahren; reiten; Fahrt	
riding	Reiten	
right	richtig; genau, direkt; (nach) rechts	
be right	Recht haben	
on the/your right	rechts, auf der/deiner rechten Seite	
river	Fluss	
road	Straße	Walk down this **road**. – Laufe diese Straße hinunter.
rock	Stein; Fels(en)	
room	Zimmer	
rope	Seil	
run	laufen, rennen	
running	Laufen, Rennen	

S

sad	traurig	
safe	sicher	
said	Vergangenheitsform von „say“	That is what I **said**! – Das habe ich gesagt!
salad	Salat	
sale	(Aus)verkauf	
sari	Sari (gewickeltes Gewand indischer Frauen)	
Saturday	Samstag	
sausage	Wurst, Würstchen	
saw	Vergangenheitsform von „see“	I **saw** your brother in the park. – Ich sah deinen Bruder im Park.
say	sagen	
say goodbye	sich verabschieden	

scared	verängstigt	
scarf/scarves	Schal/Schals	1 **scarf** – 2 **scarves**
scary	Furcht erregend, unheimlich	
scary film	Horrorfilm	
scene	Szene	
school	Schule	
school magazine	Schulzeitung, Schülerzeitung	
science	(Natur)wissenschaft	
scientific	(natur)wissenschaftlich	
score a goal	ein Tor schießen	They **scored a goal**! – Sie haben ein Tor geschossen!
Scotland	Schottland	
Scottish	Schottisch; schottisch	
scream	schreien; kreischen	
sea	Meer; See	
search	(durch)suchen	
seat	(Sitz)platz	
second	zweite(r, s); Sekunde	
see	sehen	
see you	bis dann, bis bald	**See you** tomorrow! – Bis morgen!
seen	siehe „see"	
sell	verkaufen	
seller	Verkäufer/in	
send	(zu)schicken	
sentence	Satz	
sentence part	Satzteil	
seven	sieben	My sister is **seven** years old. – Meine Schwester ist sieben Jahre alt.
seventeen	siebzehn	
shadow	Schatten	
shamrock	Klee(blatt)	
share	teilen	
sharing	Teilen	
she	sie	
she'll (= she will)	sie wird	
shield	(Schutz)schild	
shine	scheinen (*Sonne*)	
ship	Schiff	
shoe	Schuh	
shop	Geschäft, Laden	
shopping centre	Einkaufszentrum	
short	kurz	
should	sollte/müsste	
shouldn't (= should not)	sollte(st, n, t) nicht	You **shouldn't** forget your homework. – Du solltest deine Hausaufgaben nicht vergessen.
shout	schreien, rufen	
show	zeigen	
show off	angeben; zeigen, präsentieren	Stop **showing off**! – Hör auf anzugeben!

sight	Sehenswürdigkeit	
sign	Zeichen; (Straßen-/ Verkehrs)schild	
silly	dumm; albern	
sing	singen	
singer	Sänger/in	
single room	Einzelzimmer	I would like to reserve a **single room**, please. – Ich möchte gern ein Einzelzimmer reservieren.
single (ticket)	Einzelfahrkarte	
sister	Schwester	
sit	sitzen	
six	sechs	
sixteen	sechzehn	
sixty	sechzig	
skateboard	Skateboard; skaten, Skateboard fahren	
skateboarding	Skateboardfahren	
skating	Schlittschuhlaufen; Rollschuhlaufen	
skeleton	Skelett	He dressed up as a **skeleton**. – Er hat sich als Skelett verkleidet.
sleep in	ausschlafen	
slowly	langsam	
small	klein	
smart	schlau; schick	
smile	lächeln	
smoke signal	Rauchzeichen	
so	deshalb; also	
soap	Seife	
solar-powered	solarbetrieben, mit Sonnenenergie betrieben	a **solar-powered** light – eine solarbetriebene Leuchte
sold	Vergangenheitsform von „sell“	
some	einige; etwas	
someone	jemand	
something	etwas	
sometimes	manchmal	
soon	bald	
sorry	Verzeihung!, Entschuldigung!; Wie bitte?	
sound	klingen, sich anhören; Geräusch, Klang, Ton	
soup	Suppe	
soup of the day	Tagessuppe	What is the **soup of the day**? – Was ist die Tagessuppe?
space	Platz; Weltraum	
spade	Spaten; Schaufel	
sparkling	mit Kohlensäure	
speak	sprechen, reden	
special	besondere(r, s), speziell; Spezial; Sonderausgabe	
speech bubble	Sprechblase	Read the **speech bubble**. – Lies die Sprechblase.

spend	ausgeben (*Geld*); verbringen (*Zeit*)	
spinach	Spinat	
sponsored run	Sponsorenlauf	
spooky	unheimlich, schaurig	
sports centre	Sportcenter	
sports club	Sportverein	
sports event	Sportveranstaltung	There is a **sports event** at school next week. – Es gibt nächste Woche eine Sportveranstaltung an der Schule.
sports ground	Sportplatz	
sports hall	Sporthalle	
sports	Sport(art)	
squeeze	drücken	
stage	Bühne	
stall	(Verkaufs)stand	
stamp	Briefmarke	
star	Stern	
stare at sb/sth	jdn/etw anstarren	
start	anfangen, beginnen	
start	Anfang, Beginn	
starter	Vorspeise	
station	Bahnhof; Station	Where is the **station**? – Wo ist der Bahnhof?
stay	bleiben; wohnen; Aufenthalt	
step	Stufe; Schritt; treten	
stick	Stock; kleben	
still	(immer) noch, noch immer	
Stone Age	Steinzeit	
storm	Sturm	
story	Geschichte, Erzählung	
straight (on)	gerade(aus)	
street	Straße	
street festival	Straßenfest	
strong	stark	My mum is very **strong**. – Meine Mama ist sehr stark.
student	Schüler/in	
study	lernen	
stuff	Zeug; Sachen	
style	(Musik)stil	
successful	erfolgreich	
such	solche(r,s)	
such a/an ...	so ein/e	
suddenly	plötzlich, auf einmal	
sugar	Zucker	
sugary	zuckerhaltig	You shouldn't drink many **sugary** drinks. – Du solltest nicht so viele zuckerhaltige Getränke trinken.
summer	Sommer	
summer holiday	Sommerurlaub, Sommerferien	
sun	Sonne	
Sunday	Sonntag	
sunglasses	Sonnenbrille	

sunny	sonnig	
sunshine	Sonnenschein	
supermarket	Supermarkt	I am going to the **supermarket**. – Ich gehe zum Supermarkt.
sure	sicher	

surprised	überrascht	
survey	Untersuchung, Umfrage	
survival kit	Überlebensausrüstung	
swam	Vergangenheitsform von „swim“	
sweet	Süßigkeit	I have brought some **sweets**. – Ich habe Süßigkeiten mitgebracht.
swim	schwimmen	
swimming	Schwimmen	
swimming pool	Schwimmbecken, -bad	
swimwear	Badebekleidung	
sword	Schwert	

T

table	Tisch; Tabelle	
tail	Schwanz	
take	(mit)nehmen; brauchen	
take a look (at)	einen Blick werfen (auf)	**Take a look at** the picture. – Wirf einen Blick auf das Bild.
take away	wegbringen	
take down	abnehmen, abmachen, entfernen	
take part (in)	teilnehmen (an)	
take photos	Bilder machen, fotografieren	
take place	stattfinden	
taken	siehe „take“	He has **taken** his medicine. – Er hat seine Medikamente genommen.
talk (to)	sprechen/reden/sich unterhalten (mit)	
target task	Zielaufgabe	
taste	schmecken	
tasty	schmackhaft, lecker	
taught	Vergangenheitsform von „teach“	
tea	Tee	
teach	unterrichten; beibringen	
team captain	Mannschaftskapitän/in	
telephone	Telefon	
television	Fernseher; Fernsehen	
tell	erzählen	**Tell** me a story. – Erzähle mir eine Geschichte.
ten	zehn	
test	prüfen, testen; Prüfung; Test; Klassenarbeit	
text message	SMS, Kurznachricht	
textile	Stoff, Gewebe; Textilien	
Thai	thailändisch	

than	als	
thank you	danke	**Thank you** for your help! – Danke für deine Hilfe!
thanks	danke	
thanks a lot	vielen Dank	
that	dass; der/die/das	
that time	damals, zu dieser Zeit	
that's (= that is)	das ist	
the	der/die/das	
their	ihr(e)	
them	sie, ihnen	
theme	Thema; Lektion, Kapitel	
then	dann, danach	
there	dort, da	
there are	da sind; es gibt	
there is	da ist; es gibt	**There is** a book on my desk. – Auf meinem Schreibtisch ist ein Buch.
there's (= there is)	da ist; es gibt	
these days	zurzeit	
these (pl of this)	diese	
they	sie	
thing	Ding, Gegenstand, Sache	
think	denken, glauben, meinen	What do you **think**? – Was denkst du?
think of	denken an; sich ausdenken	
thirteen	dreizehn	
thirty	dreißig	
this	diese(r, s); das	
this one	diese(r, s)	
thistle	Distel	
three	drei	
through	durch	
Thursday	Donnerstag	
tick	abhaken, ankreuzen	
ticket machine	Fahrkartenautomat	We need to buy a ticket from the **ticket machine**. – Wir müssen eine Fahrkarte am Fahrkartenautomat kaufen.
ticket office	Fahrkartenschalter	
tidy	aufräumen	
time	(Uhr)zeit	
timetable	Stundenplan; Fahrplan	
tip	Tipp	
tired	müde	
to	in, nach, zu, an; um zu; mit; für	
toast	toasten, rösten	
today	heute	
together	zusammen, gemeinsam	
toilet	Toilette; Klo	
told	Vergangenheitsform von „tell"	
tomato/tomatoes	Tomate/Tomaten	1 **tomato** – 2 **tomatoes**
tomorrow	morgen	
too	zu; auch	

took	Vergangenheitsform von „take“
tooth/teeth	Zahn/Zähne
toothbrush	Zahnbürste
toothpaste	Zahnpasta
top	Spitze
at the top	oben, am oberen Ende (von), an der Spitze (von)
torch	Taschenlampe, Fackel
tourist information centre	Touristeninformations-zentrum
tower	Turm
town	Stadt
toy	Spielzeug
toy animal	Plüschtier
train	trainieren; Zug, Eisenbahn
train station	Bahnhof
trainer	Turnschuh
transport	transportieren, befördern
travel	reisen
trip	Ausflug; Reise, Fahrt
trophy	Trophäe; Preis
trouble	Schwierigkeiten
true	wahr, richtig
try	(aus)probieren, versuchen
try on	anprobieren
tulip	Tulpe
turn	sich drehen; abbiegen
twelve	zwölf
twenty	zwanzig
two	zwei

Do you have a **torch** with you? – Hast du eine Taschenlampe dabei?

Where are my **trainers**? – Wo sind meine Turnschuhe?

Would you like to **try** the shoes **on**? – Möchtest du die Schuhe anprobieren?

U

ugly	hässlich
UK (= United Kingdom)	Vereinigtes Königreich
underline	unterstreichen
understand	verstehen
unhappy	unglücklich
unicorn	Einhorn
university	Universität
up	(nach) oben; hinauf
up and away	auf und davon
upload	(hoch)laden
us	uns
USA (= United States of America)	USA, Vereinigte Staaten von Amerika
use	benutzen
user manual	Benutzerhandbuch
usual	üblich, normal

Underline the words you know. – Unterstreiche die Wörter, die du kennst.

V

vampire	Vampir/in	
van	Wagen, Transporter	
vegetable	Gemüse	Broccoli is a **vegetable**. – Brokkoli ist ein Gemüse.
vegetarian	Vegetarier/in; vegetarisch	
versus	gegen	
very	sehr	
video game	Videospiel	
Viking	Wikinger/in	
village	Dorf	I live in a small **village**. – Ich wohne in einem kleinen Dorf.
visit	besuchen; Besuch	
visitor	Besucher/in	
voice	Stimme	
volcano	Vulkan	

W

wait (for)	warten (auf)	
waiter	Bedienung, Kellner/in	
walk	gehen, laufen	
walk the dog	den Hund ausführen	
wall	Wand	
want	wollen	
was	Vergangenheitsform von „be“	I **was** tired. – Ich war müde.
wash	(sich) waschen	
watch	beobachten; anschauen	
water carrier	Wasserträger	
water	Wasser	
wave	winken	
way	Weg	
we	wir	
we'll (= we will)	wir werden	**We'll** see. – Wir werden sehen.
we're (= we are)	wir sind	
we've (= we have)	wir haben	
wear	tragen	
weather	Wetter	
week	Woche	
weekend	Wochenende	
at the weekend	am Wochenende	
well	nun (ja), tja	
Welsh	Walisisch; walisisch	
went	Vergangenheitsform von „go“	
were	Vergangenheitsform von „be“	We **were** happy. – Wir waren glücklich.
what	welche(r, s); was	
What about ...?	Was ist mit ...?, Wie wäre es mit ...?	
what's (= what is)	was ist	

What's on?	Was ist los?, Was steht an?	
What's wrong?	Was ist los?	
wheelchair	Rollstuhl	
when	wann; wenn; als	
where	wo(hin)	
which	welche(r, s); der/die/das	
while	Weile	
white	weiß	
who	wer; der/die/das	**Who** are you? – Wer bist du?
why	warum	
wife/wives	Ehefrau/Ehefrauen	
will	werden	I **will** – ich werde you **will** – du wirst he/she/it **will** – er/sie/es wird we **will** – wir werden you **will** – ihr werdet they **will** – sie werden
win	gewinnen	
window	Fenster	
winning	Gewinn-, siegreich, Sieger-	
winning goal	Siegtreffer	
witch	Hexe	
with	mit; bei	
without	ohne	
woman/women	Frau/Frauen	1 **woman** – 2 **women**
won	Vergangenheitsform von „win“	
wonderful	wunderbar, wundervoll	
wood	Holz	
word	Wort	
wordsearch	Wortsuchrätsel	
wore	Vergangenheitsform von „wear“	
work	arbeiten	Where does your mum **work**? – Wo arbeitet deine Mama?
working	Arbeiten, Arbeit	
world	Welt; Erde	
world's best	weltbeste(r, s)	
worn	siehe „wear“	
worried	beunruhigt, besorgt	
worry	sich Sorgen machen; Sorge	
would	würde(st, n, t)	
would like (to)	möchte (gern)	I **would like to** listen to music. – Ich würde gern Musik hören.
wouldn't (= would not)	würde(st, n, t) nicht	
write	schreiben	
write down	aufschreiben	
wrong	falsch	
wrote	Vergangenheitsform von „write“	

Y

yeah	ja	
year	Jahr; Jahrgang(sstufe)	I'm in **year** 7. – Ich bin in der 7. Klasse.
yes	ja	
yesterday	gestern	
not yet	noch nicht	
yoghurt	Joghurt	
Yorkshire pudding	eine Art Gebäck als Beilage zu Fleischgerichten	
you	du, dich, dir, Sie, Ihnen; ihr, euch	
you're (= you are)	du bist; ihr seid	
You're welcome.	Gern geschehen., Bitte.	
young	jung	I have a **younger** sister. – Ich habe eine jüngere Schwester.
your	dein(e); euer/eure; Ihr(e)	
youth club	Jugendzentrum	
yummy	lecker	

Z

zip	Reißverschluss

The days of the week

Monday
Tuesday
Wednesday
Thursday
Friday
Saturday
Sunday

The months

January	July
February	August
March	September
April	October
May	November
June	December

Numbers

0	zero
1	one
2	two
3	three
4	four
5	five
6	six
7	seven
8	eight
9	nine
10	ten
11	eleven
12	twelve
13	thirteen
14	fourteen
15	fifteen
16	sixteen
17	seventeen
18	eighteen
19	nineteen
20	twenty
21	twenty-one
22	twenty-two
23	twenty-three
24	twenty-four
25	twenty-five
26	twenty-six
27	twenty-seven
28	twenty-eight
29	twenty-nine
30	thirty
31	thirty-one

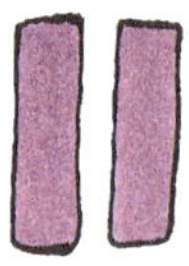

40	forty
50	fifty
60	sixty
70	seventy
80	eighty
90	ninety
100	one hundred

1st	first
2nd	second
3rd	third
4th	fourth
5th	fifth
6th	sixth
7th	seventh
8th	eighth
9th	ninth
10th	tenth
11th	eleventh
12th	twelfth
13th	thirteenth
14th	fourteenth
15th	fifteenth
16th	sixteenth
17th	seventeenth
18th	eighteenth
19th	nineteenth
20th	twentieth
21st	twenty-first
22nd	twenty-second
...	
30th	thirtieth
31st	thirty-first

Trackliste

Alle Audiodateien findest du unter:

www.westermann.de/webcode

Gib den folgenden Webcode ein:

WES-149141-001

Oder scanne den QR-Code ein:

Dann kannst du die Dateien herunterladen.

Theme 1: Are you fit?

Keeping fit

1. 7 A sports event
2. 8 A friendly match

Eating habits

3. 1 In the cafeteria
4. 3 Good for you?
5. 4 Lunch at school
6. 9 Eating out
7. 11 Choose an activity
8. 12 In a restaurant

Optional: ⊞ Language special

9. 2 That's cool!

Theme 2: What's on near you?

Things we can do

10. 1 Different places
11. 7 A chat
12. 10 I'll take it
13. 11 At the car boot sale
14. 12 Buying and selling

Street festivals

15. 2 The Jorvik Viking Festival
16. 3b A day at the festival
17. 3d A day at the festival
18. 9a A phone call
19. 9b A phone call

Theme 3: You're not alone

Robinson Crusoe

20. 2 Your survival kit
21. 9a I'd like to know ...
22. 9c I'd like to know ...
23. 14 Target task: Your dream island

Dealing with problems

24. 1a Letters to Holly
25. 1c Letters to Holly
26. 7 Sandeep and his family
27. 10 Talking to a friend
28. 16 Target task: Give a helping hand

Theme 4: Everyday science

Digital world

29. 1 A very short history of communication
30. 5 A new experience
31. 6a Sharing information
32. 6c Sharing information

Inventions

33. 1 Inventions
34. 9 The Science and Industry Museum in Manchester

Optional: ⊞ The UK and Ireland

35. 3 Scotland

Theme 5: Up and away

Planning a holiday

36. 3 Making plans
37. 4 Talking to Dad
38. 5 At the station
39. 8 Station announcements
40. 9 At the ticket office

Let's go to Scotland!

41. 1 First day in Edinburgh
42. 3a Giving directions
43. 3c Giving directions
44. 6 Making a reservation
45. 7 A trip to Loch Ness
46. 8 The story in short

QUELLENVERZEICHNIS

Audiodateien

Tonstudio: TEFL AUDIO, London; Produzent: John Green, Ton: Tim Woolf

Gesprochen von: Heather Nichol; Alex Wingfield; Nigel Greaves; Jenny Bryce; Ewan Goddard; Steven France; Harriet Kershaw; Roger May; Paul Panting; Penelope Rawlins; Claire Morgan; Clare Louise Connolly and Richard Pearce

Bildquellen

|akg-images GmbH, Berlin: 69.4, 69.5. |Alamy Stock Photo, Abingdon/Oxfordshire: Alternative Occasions 42.1, 42.2; Dagnall, Ian 80.5; Furian, Peter Hermes 76.1, 77.1, 78.1, 79.1, 80.1; Grigorjeva, Anna 6.1; Ian Dagnall, Ian 78.6, 90.2; John Peter Photography 78.5; Manor Photography 36.1; Matthew Noble Travel 80.6; Photogenic 79.2; Pictures Now 60.2; Steve Allen Travel Photography 81.4; Teague, Steve 74.2; Walmsley, Alan 36.3; Waugh, Mark 72.5. |Alamy Stock Photo (RMB), Abingdon/Oxfordshire: Bailey-Cooper Photography 90.3; Geoff du Feu 31.1; Hipix 68.2, 70.1; Paik Photography 31.3; © AA World Travel Library 73.2; © AlamyCelebrity 13.2; © Paul Francis 77.3, 77.5. |Colourbox.com, Odense: 81.1. |Cummins, Emily: 71.1, 71.2. |Druwe & Polastri, Cremlingen/Weddel: 45.6. |Fischer, Knoblauch & Co. Medienproduktionsgesellschaft mbH, München: 17.1, 17.2, 17.3. |fotolia.com, New York: 300dpi 68.7; adisa 33.7; Birgit Reitz-Hofmann 45.5; Cline, Dusty 33.9; dino4ka2020 - 80.2; djama 45.3; Emin Ozkan 68.12, 70.3; froto 45.1; Gstudio Group 68.9, 70.4; JiSign 33.1, 33.2; JulietPhotography 92.1; moonrun 5.1, 13.1, 73.1, 93.1; psdesign1 60.1; rdnzl 15.3; RRF 45.10; Rtimages 14.1; svort 45.9; Tribalstar 68.6; TrudiDesign 15.4; V. Kramin 68.13; © Joe Gough 18.2; © sergio37_120 68.1, 68.5. |Getty Images, München: Hulton Archive 69.2; Mcbride, Joe 8.1; Underwood Archives 69.6. |Gough, James, Braunschweig: 75.1. |Gray, Caitlin, Braunschweig: 43.1. |Hamill, Aisling, Braunschweig: 43.2. |Imago, Berlin: Colorsport 10.2; Simka, Darius/ regios24 10.1. |Interfoto, München: Mary Evans / Photo Researchers 69.3. |iStockphoto.com, Calgary: Alesikka 76.3; armvector 76.2; bebuntoon 33.3; deliormanli, mustafa 68.11; DEREKMcDOUGALL 78.4; Fredex8 81.3; freeman98589 60.3; JazzIRT 68.10; JoeDunckley 76.5; johnnyscriv 33.5; L-Hamilton 93.2; ma-k 15.2; Matt84 93.3; Michael Flippo 45.7; monkeybusinessimages Titel; nimblewit 45.4; PILIPIPA 52.1; Rouzes 45.8; subjug 15.5; Teresa Gueck 18.3; Veronaa 81.2; visual7 81.5; winyuu 33.4, 33.8. |mauritius images GmbH, Mittenwald: blickwinkel / Protze, Olaf 80.4; BY 79.4, 80.3; Science Source 61.1; Science Source / New York Public Library 60.4; Warburton-Lee, John / Sweene, Jane 79.3. |PantherMedia GmbH (panthermedia.net), München: mr_Brightside 74.1; rrrneumi 50.1. |Picture-Alliance GmbH, Frankfurt a.M.: 91020 69.1. |School of Physics and Astronomy, Manchester: Reproduced with the permission of the University of Manchester 61.2. |Science & Society Picture Library, London: MOSI, Manchester 72.1; © Museum of Science and Industry 72.3, 72.4; © Science Museum 72.2. |Shutterstock.com, New York: Billy Read 78.2; Chukov 68.4; fim.design 63.1, 63.2, 63.3, 63.4, 63.5, 63.6; Kalina, Alexander 8.2; MarkUK97 77.2, 77.4; Seregam 45.2; StoryTime Studio 63.8. |stock.adobe.com, Dublin: Andronov, Leonid 76.6; Andy 32.2; annanahabed 63.7; Apart Foto 68.8, 70.2; Bueckert, Axel 68.3; Charlotte 78.3; Christian B. 44.2; denisgorelkin 90.5, 90.6; EdNurg 33.6; Fidan 32.1; fotomowo 67.1, 67.2, 67.3; kebox 67.4; kevma20 74.3; Krakenimages. com 61.4; Lukassek 90.4; michaeljung 31.2; mrnai 76.4; Mucha, Thomas 60.5; nito 44.1; Prostock-studio 53.1; Rixie 77.6; snyGGG 74.4; stockphoto-graf 15.6; stocksolutions 90.1; Syda Productions 59.1; Thaut Images 82.1; UJac 18.1; Urupong 61.3; walentine 33.10; waranyu 53.2; wolfelarry 15.1. |Wefringhaus, Klaus, Braunschweig: 26.1. |York Archaeological Trust, York, North Yorkshire: 36.2. |Zwick, Joachim, Gießen: 142.1.

Textquellen

58 – „Don't worry, be happy" © Bobby McFerrin 1988, Prob Noblem Music

[redacted] (Railway)
Station (Underground)
Park / open space
0 mile 1/4 1/2
0 km 0,5 1
Hendon
London
Maida Vale
Primrose Hill
Regent's Park
London Zoo
Prince Albert Road
Grand Union Canal
Camden Town
Camden High St.
Hampstead Road
Albany Street
Pancras Road
King's Cross Stn.
St. Pancras Stn.
Euston Stn.
Euston Road
Wellington Road
Maida Vale
Grove End Road
Park Road
Marylebone Stn.
Mme. Tussaud's
Marylebone Road
Edgware Road
Westway A 40 (M)
Baker Street
Marylebone
Bloomsbury
University
Brit. Museum
Finsbury
Gray's Inn Road
Theobald's Road
Holborn
Clerkenwell
Old Street
City Road
Moorgate
Liverpool Street Stn.
Bishopsgate
City
High Holborn
Kingsway
City Thames-Link Stn.
St. Paul's Cathedral
Fleet Street
Cannon Street
Fenchurch Street Stn.
Cannon Street Stn.
Upper Thames
Tower of London
Tower Bridge
London Bridge
London Bridge Stn.
River Thames
Millenium Bridge
Blackfriars Bridge
Blackfriars Road
Southwark Street
Borough High Street
Southwark
Elephant and Castle Stn.
Waterloo East Stn.
Waterloo International Stn.
Waterloo Road
Waterloo Bridge
London Eye
Victoria Embankment
Strand
Aldwych
Covent Garden
Charing Cross
Charing Cross Road
Soho
Piccadilly Circus
Regent Street
New Bond Street
Oxford Street
Wigmore Street
Mayfair
Piccadilly
Pall Mall
Mall
Horse Guards
Whitehall
No. 10 Downing Street
Westminster Bridge
Big Ben
Westminster Hall
Houses of Parliament
Westminster Abbey
Westminster Bridge Road
Lambeth Palace Rd.
Lambeth Bridge
Lambeth Road
Westminster
Victoria Street
Victoria Stn.
Vauxhall Bridge
Buckingham Palace
Grosvenor Place
Green Park
The St. James's Park
Hyde Park
Park Lane
The Serpentine
Kensington Gardens
Round Pond
Bayswater Road
Bayswater
Paddington Stn.
Chepstow Rd.
Notting Hill
Pembridge
Kensington Road
Knightsbridge
Royal Albert Hall
Museums
Natural History Museum
Brompton Road
Sloane Street
Cromwell Road
Av. Avenue
Cl. Close
Cr. Crescent
Dr. Drive
Gds. Gardens
Gro. Grove
La. Lane
Pl. Place
Rd. Road
Sq. Square
St. Street
Terr. Terrace
Vs. Villas
Hawley Rd.
Castleh. Rd.
Camden Road Stn.
Camden Road
Camden Street
markets
Regent's Canal
Kentish Town Road
Royal College Street
Saint Pancras Way
Bayham Street
Parkway
Delancey Street
0 100 200 300 m